SEVEN DA[YS]

April 10, 2009: A woman [at the] Westin Hotel in Boston, M[assachusetts immedi-]ately identifies a tall, blond, clean-cut man as her attacker in surveillance photos released by the police . . . 11 . . . 12 . . . 13 . . .

April 14: The body of Julissa Brisman is found in a pool of blood at Boston's Marriott Copley Place Hotel; that same blond man is captured again on the hotel's security cameras . . . 15 . . .

April 16: An exotic dancer is bound in an attempted robbery at a Holiday Inn Express in Warwick, Rhode Island; for the third time in a week, investigators obtain clear photographs of the same man. Who is he? Police know one thing for sure—he's picking out his victims from Craigslist, the online bulletin board.

April 21, 2009: Philip Markoff is charged with armed robbery, kidnapping, and the murder of Julissa Brisman. . . .

"[This] meticulously researched and accessible narrative looks at the story from every angle. . . . Cramer and LaRosa have painstakingly sifted through the available evidence, yet the story is far from over. With Markoff's murder trial to come, more revelations are sure to follow."

—*Boston Globe*

"[A] fantastic new release from the *48 Hours Mystery* series. . . . An explosive true-crime book."

—True Crime Book Reviews

This title is also available as an eBook

The Deadly Crime Spree of the Craigslist Killer

Seven Days of Rage

Paul LaRosa and Maria Cramer

POCKET STAR BOOKS

New York   London   Toronto   Sydney

Pocket Star Books
A Division of Simon & Schuster, Inc.
1230 Avenue of the Americas
New York, NY 10020

This book is a work of fiction. Names, characters, places, and incidents either are products of the author's imagination or are used fictitiously. Any resemblance to actual events or locales or persons, living or dead, is entirely coincidental.

First Pocket Star Books paperback edition June 2010

POCKET STAR BOOKS and colophon are registered trademarks of Simon & Schuster, Inc.

For information about special discounts for bulk purchases, please contact Simon & Schuster Special Sales at 1-866-506-1949 or business@simonandschuster.com

The Simon & Schuster Speakers Bureau can bring authors to your live event. For more information or to book an event contact the Simon & Schuster Speakers Bureau at 1-866-248-3049 or visit our website at www.simonspeakers.com.

Designed by Ruth Lee-Mui
Jacket design by Jae Song
Jacket photograph: Boston, Chris Lacroix/Stock.Xchng; Julissa Brisman, © Splash News; Philip Markoff, AP Photo/Mark Garfinkel.

10 9 8 7 6 5 4 3 2 1

ISBN 978 1-4391-7239-1
ISBN 978 1-9821-5990-0 (pbk)
ISBN 978 1-4391-7287-2 (ebook)

*Dedicated to all family members and friends who
must live with the devastating effects of
the murder of their loved ones . . .*

Contents

I've seen the future, brother: it is murder.

— LEONARD COHEN

Prologue

Secrets

On May 31, 2007, a young college graduate fired up his computer and took the plunge. He entered his credit card information and just like that was granted access to the erotic online website known as Alt.com. Alt.com, for the uninitiated, is Match.com on steroids—and naked. Got a fetish or an outlandish desire that needs attending? Then Alt.com is for you. *Alt* is short for *alternative*, and the website bills itself as *Your online adult personals, BDSM* [meaning bondage, domination, and sadomasochism], *Leather & Fetish Community.* Most Americans know nothing about Alt.com, but it claims to have nearly three million active members who consider it a way of life, a balls-to-the-wall dating site where members post photos, personals, and all manner of erotic exchanges.

And on the last day of May 2007, this young man began to pursue such an alternative lifestyle—in secret. Once granted access, he created his online persona, calling himself sexaddict53885, and posted a photo of his naked torso and, as is de rigueur on the site, his erect penis. Then he typed in his basic stats:

Birthday: February 12, 1986
Hair color: Blond
Hair length: Short
Eyes: Blue
Height: 6 feet, 4 inches, 193–195 cm
Race: Caucasian
Lives in: Boston, Massachusetts

I think about ALT lifestyle: All the time
Role: Submissive
Level of Experience: I am new at this

He listed some of the sexual activities he enjoyed, including anal sex, wearing a collar and leash, and cross-dressing. Then he wrote up his profile: *I am currently a graduate student looking to experiment with the BDSM lifestyle . . . I am very interested in being dominated, and made to do different things.*

Alt.com encourages users to list their "ideal person" and sexaddict53885 wrote: *I am looking for anyone open minded try [sic] new fetishes or show me what you know. I enjoy women . . . but I really want to meet a tv/tg/ts for friendship and experimentation. I am looking for doms and switch's [sic], but I am open to experimenting with subs.*

To translate, *tv/tg/ts* is shorthand for *transvestite, transgender,* and *transsexual. Doms* are those who dominate, and *switchs* are those who go back and forth between being dominant and submissive.

With his profile filled in according to his deepest, most secret desires, sexaddict53885 began to cruise the site and build his list of "friends"—other Alt.com members who caught his fancy. The "friends" he chose were both male and female, and included a variety of cross-dressers, transgenders, and dominatrices, some of whom posted photos of themselves engaged in sexual activity. He also chose people he could possibly meet, and most of his friends were close to his stated location of Boston or were from upstate New York around Syracuse.

It would have been unthinkable for any of sexaddict-53885's real-world friends to imagine him being involved in something like this; they did not know this side of him, the thrill-seeking side. In fact, there was a lot about him that his friends didn't know: his love of gambling, his cruising of the erotic personals for both men and women on Craigslist, and the sexually charged emails he exchanged with men who dressed as women. In sexaddict53885's normal life, he was nothing like this—as he himself said in his profile, he was a graduate student. But having this secret life must have been a thrill in itself.

Who was this new graduate, sexaddict53885? The username, the torso photo, the height and weight, even the birthday, all match the identifying details of Philip Markoff. In May 2007, Markoff had just graduated from the University at Albany-SUNY and was about to enter the Boston University School of Medicine. There was nothing illegal about his secret life, nothing at all, but, if the police are correct, his joining that website and indulging his alternative lifestyle might have been the beginning of Markoff's descent into a deadly game of thrill seeking that ended in murder.

1

A Sweet Blonde

It was Trisha Leffler's first visit to Boston. Her flight from Las Vegas landed at around 6 p.m. on April 9, and she caught a cab to the hotel she'd booked on Hotwire. com—the Westin Copley Place in Boston's upscale Back Bay, a mecca of shopping for locals and tourists alike. But Trisha wasn't in Boston to shop, see the Red Sox, or walk the Freedom Trail. She was there to *work*, and after settling into her room—taking a shower and throwing her dirty clothes on the floor—she logged onto her new computer and placed an ad on Craigslist.

For the uninitiated, Craigslist.org is an online bulletin board and the go-to site for just about anything you might desire. For anyone under thirty, it's a way of life, a permanent way station on the Internet to be checked whenever you're looking for an apartment, a job, a coffee table, a book club, a nanny, or a hookup. It's a friend when you're bored, a counselor when you're blue, a release when you're sexually frustrated. It is its own universe. Craigslist is not only *the* dominant online bulletin board—it's the *only* one most people can name. More so than even Google or Microsoft, Craigslist is master of its domain.

The ad Trisha posted that evening was simple but not direct. It meandered around the main point but, if you came across it, listed in the board's erotic services section, you knew what was being offered. "It basically said, if you'd like to come spend some time with a sweet blonde, give me a call so we can spend some time together," Trisha recalled. "That's basically the ins and outs of it."

Trisha, a twenty-nine-year-old resident of Las Vegas with a criminal record for soliciting prostitution, put her cell phone number in the ad, then sat back and waited. She'd come a long way from her Mormon roots. Trisha, a bleached blonde, was raised a Mormon in Utah, but by the time she was in her early twenties, she was living full-time in Las Vegas. She began to sell her body, but it wasn't always easy, not when the next batch of younger and more enticing hookers arrived almost daily. So she branched out, and sometimes hit the open road. When she got some money together, she would travel to a different city based on two criteria: it had to be new and interesting, and it had to provide some work.

That's how she found herself in Boston on the evening of April 9. It was now late on Thursday night, bleeding into Friday morning, but it was a *drinking* night, and for certain guys—alone, or bored with their wives and girlfriends—it was the perfect night to spend some time alone in a hotel room with a "sweet blonde" who made no demands. And Trisha is a nice person, if a little lost in the world. Her best friend seems to be her tiny Pomeranian named Pixie. She's put on a few extra pounds over the years, but her calling card is her easy-going nature, and it's not hard to understand why men enjoy spending time with her. She's vulnerable, agreeable, and quick to laugh.

She waited for the call that was sure to come, because if Trisha knew one thing, it was this: men in Boston were no different from men everywhere else. Sure enough, her cell phone rang. A few guys were interested but there was nothing definite. And then a man called who sounded more serious. Trisha could tell from his questions.

What part of town are you in?

Copley Square.

In a hotel?

Yes, the Westin.

Okay.

What kind of work do you do?

I'm a student.

Okay, so you wanna come by?

Yes.

Trisha had noted in her ad that she had different rates. You could spend a half hour or an hour with her, your choice. "He asked me how much it was for the half hour and the hour and I told him it was two hundred dollars for the hour," she said.

Okay, an hour sounds fine.

Okay, so call when you get to the hotel and I'll tell you what floor I'm on.

Trisha maintains that there was no talk of sex, and no explicit promises were exchanged. "He was just gonna pay me for my time," she said. "And about a half hour or twenty minutes later, he called me when he got to the Westin."

Hey, I'm the guy who called.

Are you here?

Yes, what floor are you on?

Thirteen.

Ah, thirteen, my lucky number.

Trisha employed the routine she always uses when meeting a client for the first time; giving the man her floor number but that's all. She meets the client at the elevator and sizes him up. "If I don't feel comfortable, then I'll just walk away from the person. That way, they don't know exactly what room number I'm in," she said. "If I'm not comfortable, I just tell 'em, 'No thanks.'"

Trisha was done up in a short black, jersey-knit dress that showed off her curves. She walked down the hall to the elevator bank, and the moment the doors opened, she liked what she saw. "He was tall, a good-looking guy," she said. "When I first laid eyes on him, I was comfortable because, you know, he was a regular-looking guy. It didn't look like he had any other tendencies other than just spend a little time and leave. I just said, 'Hi,' and he said, 'Hi,' and I motioned for him to follow me. I didn't really wanna talk out in the hallway."

The man was dressed in a black leather

coat, dark jeans, and a tan shirt. He had blond hair and light-colored eyes, and Trisha estimated that he was in his late twenties.

"So we went into the room, and as soon as I closed the door and I had turned around, he was standing there just inside the door. That's when he pulled out the gun. I immediately started shaking. My heart started beating real fast."

Trisha later said that the gun was black and "definitely not a revolver. It was a semiautomatic and it looked to be a pretty big caliber." Remaining as polite as ever, the man ordered Trisha to lie down on the floor. She knew one thing—it was best to remain calm. She did what he asked. The guy was well over six feet and towered over Trisha, who is five foot two and weighs about 135 pounds. "He put the gun back in his pocket and stepped behind me, and he kneeled on the ground with one knee in between my legs and told me to put my hands behind my back, which I did. And then he tied me up, one hand at a time."

You don't have to do all this. You don't have to

tie me up. I'll give you whatever you want. You don't have to tie me up.

If you just be quiet, no harm's gonna come to you.

At that point, the good-looking stranger pulled on a pair of black leather gloves. "In the back of my mind, I'm thinking, it's a toy and it's not loaded," she said of the gun. She was reassured by the guy's gentlemanly manner. "He was very calm. He didn't tell me to shut up, he told me to be quiet. I guess you could call him polite. He didn't call me names or swear at me."

Where's your money?

In my purse.

He mistakenly picked up Trisha's makeup case from the desk.

In here?

No, my purse is in the top drawer of the entertainment center.

She had $800 in cash. "He immediately went for the money, took it out, and put it in his pocket. Then he knelt down on the floor and rifled through my purse. He took out my wallet, taking each credit card out, and asking me what kind of credit cards they were."

It was Trisha's habit to carry gift cards. Some had money on them, some did not, but she liked to carry them so that if she was ever in a bind, she could call a friend to put extra cash on the cards. For her, it was easier than carrying regular credit cards. She did have one bank debit card, which caught the man's eye.

What's your pin number?

"My adrenaline was rushing so much, I couldn't think of a lie, so I gave him the pin number."

That better be the pin number or there's gonna be a problem later.

This tall guy, who had remained calm throughout the robbery, put all the cards and Trisha's wallet in his pocket. Suddenly, she was worried, not so much about getting killed but about getting home. Without her ID, getting back to Vegas—getting anywhere—was going to be a major hassle. It's funny the things that go through one's mind at a time like this. Without thinking, Trisha blurted out:

Can you please leave me my ID so I can get home?

"And he took it out and studied it for a good minute like he was memorizing my address and then threw it down with all the rest of the stuff."

So far, so good, thought Trisha. She decided to push her luck.

Can you please leave me at least one credit card?

I thought you said there wasn't any money on them.

There's not but I can have people put money on it so I can get home.

Which one do you want?

The one ending in 7649.

The stranger cleverly slipped that one into his pocket and threw down a different one. Then he picked up a camera—a Sony Cybershot—lying with her stuff and asked Trisha if it was hers. It was. She didn't see him take it right then and there, but later she realized it was gone. Now that the guy had all her money, her two American Express gift cards, and her debit card with her pin number, Trisha wondered what was next, and thinking of the possibilities made her very nervous. "I'm still shaking but his demeanor was actually pretty calm, like he had done this before. He seemed to know what to look for."

Whatever was coming, Trisha wanted to face it head-on. She was uncomfortable lying on the hotel carpet.

Is it okay if I sit up?

Okay.

He helped her sit up, but her hands remained tied behind her back.

Where's your phone?

On the table.

He took her cell phone and began going through the numbers, but he was fumbling with it.

What are you doing?

I'm erasing my number.

Can I do it for you?

No, I'll take care of it. I got it.

He still had his gloves on, and after erasing the number, he took the battery out and threw it behind the entertainment center. "He didn't want me to get to it right away," she said. "He started looking around my room a little bit but I didn't say anything to him, and then he picked up a pair of my underwear from the floor and put them in his pocket. He didn't smell them or anything. I thought it was weird but I didn't ask him what he was doing. I didn't care to know. I wanted him out."

The thong panties, left in a pile of dirty clothes, were white and cream colored and had been purchased at Victoria's Secret. "If he looked over at me then, he would have seen the smirk on my face," she said. "I was like, 'What the hell did you do that for?' "

The stranger did not see the smirk but he wasn't ready to leave. He continued to walk around the room, as if looking for something else. He examined her brand-new computer.

Is this yours?

Yes, but it's three years old. You don't want that.

He left it where it was and continued to look around.

Is there a safe in here?

Yes, but there's nothing in it.

He opened it anyway, and then kept circling the room. "I was getting antsy and I wanted him to leave. He was moving furniture around."

What are you doing?

I'm looking for something to tie you to. I need time to get out of here. Or should I just cut you loose?

Yeah, cut me loose. I won't call anyone. I'll give you time to get away.

I don't believe you.

He was playing a game of cat and mouse, and Trisha wanted out. "I started suggesting things he could tie me to, so he would leave. I said, 'What about this, what about that?' but he thought I could move those things. Finally he tied me to the bathroom door and moved away from me."

Trisha couldn't see what he was doing. "I heard him rustling in his pocket for something. I heard the zipper on my suitcase, and then he ended up putting three pieces of tape over my mouth. I noticed at that point he was not wearing gloves and I let him put the tape on me."

Days later she would realize that he had taken a second pair of her underwear, a V-shaped pink thong with black bows. It was a new pair she had bought for an upcoming photo shoot.

But at that moment, with the stranger still in her room, Trisha was not thinking about underwear. Her eyes were focused on the huge silver knife with a black handle that the stranger now had in his hand. She suspected the worst, but instead of coming in her direction, the man used the knife to cut the phone lines. "I guess he didn't want me to have a direct outlet," she said. She waited for his next move. Even after everything that had happened, she could not help noticing how tall and good-looking, how *normal* this stranger seemed. She never would have guessed that he'd be one of the problem ones. He took a long, slow look around the room.

Just stay where you are. In fifteen minutes I'll call security and tell them I heard something in the room. They'll come up and set you free.

And then the man left.

Trisha waited, tied to the bathroom door, her mouth duct-taped shut, her hands tied behind her back. He had, she said, used plastic zip ties for both hands. She did not move. She had to be sure he wasn't outside the door, waiting for her to do something. She didn't want to give him a reason to come back and kill her.

But then, after hearing nothing, "I twisted out of the ties in ten or twenty seconds. I took the tape off my mouth and crumpled it up and waited one more minute."

"I wasn't going to call the cops, but then I thought he might still be in the hotel," she said. If there was any chance of the cops or security catching him, this was it. She stepped into the hallway and looked both ways. Nothing. She grabbed her room key, ran to the nearest door, and pounded. After a moment, a man opened the door.

Trisha was still shaking. The man, a Tennessee doctor in town on business, was hesitant to open the door all the way, but Trisha begged him, "Please, I need to call security. I've just been robbed."

The man opened the door and let her in. It was 12:45 a.m. on April 10.

2

Aftermath

For the next two hours, Boston Police detectives spoke to Trisha, and, she says, they took her story seriously from the very beginning. "They roped off the room as a crime scene and brought me down to another room to interview me," she said.

Trisha's night had gone badly, but she had good luck when it came to the investigating officers. One of them was Sergeant Detective Dan Keeler, a legend on the Boston Police

Department who had closed more than two hundred murder cases in a dozen years, more than enough to earn the nickname "Mr. Homicide." Keeler made his mark at the very beginning of his career in 1980 when he leaped off the Boston University Bridge and fell sixty feet to rescue a depressed man trying to drown himself in the Charles River. Keeler wound up saving the man's life. In questioning suspects, he had an aggressive style. Over the years, Keeler had run into some static with the District Attorney's office and had been transferred out of the homicide unit, which is why he was now responding to Trisha's robbery report. Now in his late fifties, he is still a cop's cop, and he is always there for crime victims, including Trisha.

As the questioning began, Trisha was a reluctant witness who would say little more than that she was from Las Vegas. Certainly, she was leery of the police, having been arrested before. And at that point, she had no way of knowing whether that night she'd be arrested yet again.

Keeler, in his gentle but firm way, began working on her, and as one of his bosses later said, "He was the perfect guy to respond because he's very good at getting the facts from someone."

"He was very nice and understanding," Trisha said. "A great listener, and he cleared things up for me when I had questions about what was happening the night of the robbery."

When the questioning was over, Trisha was escorted back to the hotel, where management assigned her a new room on a different floor. She originally had planned to be in Boston for a week, but now she wasn't so sure. The incident had left her shaken and she knew she had been lucky to escape unscathed. The guy who robbed her had barely even touched her, except for when he tied her up with the zip ties. There had been no sexual assault, and she had suffered no physical harm. He could have done anything he wanted to but had done nothing. Thinking that maybe luck was on her side after all, she elected to stay in Boston. The robbery had not made the papers, so there was no heat on her to leave. The biggest hassle was that the cops took Trisha's cell phone and her attacker had taken most of her credit cards and money.

The next morning, she headed for police headquarters in Roxbury where she'd promised the detectives she would look at mug shots. She also wanted to get her phone back. She didn't see anyone remotely familiar in the photos but then the cops showed her some grainy still photos they'd pulled from the hotel's surveillance cameras. There was the big, blond guy with the leather coat and hat walking outside the hotel. The photo was not great but Trisha recognized the man immediately—he was the guy, she said, who had held her up less than twenty-four hours before. Investigators also told Trisha that they'd learned her attacker had used her debit card about an hour after the robbery. He'd gone to an ATM outside a nearby pizza parlor and had accessed her account using the PIN number she'd given him. It had worked fine but the joke was on him—Trisha had only $20 in her account. He withdrew it anyway.

Trisha was afraid, but she was stuck in Boston until a friend put some money on her credit card. She also wanted to recoup some of her losses.

3

A Real NYC Girl

On Monday, April 13, the day after Easter, Julissa Brisman packed a bag and boarded an Amtrak train from New York City to Boston. She had a few massage clients lined up and intended to find some new ones by placing an ad on Craigslist.

Julissa was twenty-five years old and a New Yorker through and through, and the *only* reason she was going to Boston, home of the hated Red Sox, was for work. Her parents were Dominican, but if you asked Julissa her nationality, she might very well say "New Yorker." She loved the city that much and admitted to having withdrawal symptoms when she was away too long. She let her Facebook friends know it: *AHHHH!! I miss NYC soooo much!!! I miss the rude cab drivers and Bi-polar* [sic] *weather!! Hahaha . . . lol.*

To Julissa, everything about the Big Apple was "chill"—even the noise. You had to get with it or get out of it was her reasoning, and if you so much as covered your ears when a screeching train pulled into a subway station, well, then you were so *not* a New Yorker. She loved the magical things that were always happening to her in the city, like the time she dropped her iPod onto the subway tracks, and a guy immediately jumped down to fetch it for her. That's the kind of thing that happens to very attractive young females in the city, and that was Julissa through and through. She led a fun life and was in love with her hometown. On her Facebook profile, Julissa had bragged that she was "a born and raised N.Y.C. hottie finally getting a hold of this Wonderful thing we call Life!!"

For good measure, she quoted the quintessential if semifictional New York character Carrie Bradshaw from the HBO series *Sex and the City*: "The most exciting, challenging, and significant relationship of all is the one you have with yourself. And if you find someone to love the you *you* love, well, that's just fabulous."

One thing's for sure: Julissa was not shy about exploiting her come-hither looks. A part-time model, she loved posing for photographs in bikinis, scanty clothes, and underwear. She was a little over five feet tall and weighed maybe a hundred pounds; her shape was close to perfection by nearly any man's standards. A few years earlier, when in her early twenties, she had worn her hair straight, bleached it blond, and become the ultimate New York City party girl.

That's when her good friend Sarah first crossed paths with Julissa. It was back in 2005, after Sarah posted an ad on Craigslist looking for a roommate. She agreed to let Julissa move in with her but wondered if they'd get along. Sarah said that Julissa drank way too much and loved to party. What's more, she always seemed to have a different boyfriend and would bring strangers over to the apartment for impromptu parties . . . but Sarah also said she was fun as hell.

Another of Julissa's friends, Monica, said that Julissa was "promiscuous" and would often hook up with different guys at bars and parties. But even Monica could not help loving Julissa, mainly because of the young woman's gregarious spirit: "Julissa was fun and happy. She always made jokes and laughed at life. She was generous and always had a compliment to give."

Sarah agreed. Despite Julissa's wild partying, Sarah said that Julissa grew on her and, in time, the two became inseparable. They did everything together—going to the gym, eating sushi, talking over wine, or chowing down on some of Julissa's favorite foods: strawberries, cashews, and mozzarella cheese. She had peculiar eating habits and was not above eating a pint of cookies-and-cream ice cream topped off with cashews and strawberries for breakfast.

The women had tons of laughs, and Julissa especially adored *Sex and the City*. She played a game with Sarah whereby they forced their dates to watch and endure the female-bonding series. Living with Julissa was a gas, but after living in Julissa's world for two very long years, Sarah grew weary. There were times when Julissa would be drunk all day long. Julissa seemed to have no idea of what she wanted out of life, according to Sarah. She moved out and the two drifted apart.

Julissa went her own way. She worked various odd jobs, among them as a bartender, a shoe saleswoman, and an associate in a tanning salon. She had tons of friends, and she remained close to her family—a sister ten years younger than she and their mother, Carmen, who raised her girls in an apartment up on

West 107th Street in Manhattan. Julissa told
friends she did not know her father very well.
And then there was Julissa's absolute best
friend, her tiny mixed-breed dog named Coco
Chanel (despite its name, the half silk terrier,
half Chihuahua was male). "She would often
say, 'I love Coco more than all of my boyfriends combined,' " her friend Mark Pines remembers.

Pines, sixty, a large man who was fiercely
protective of Julissa, became her trusted advisor
after they met when Julissa was twenty years old.
Pines held an open audition for a video shoot,
and when Julissa walked in, he decided on the
spot that she was perfect. He eventually featured
her in a public service announcement he's still
trying to get the City of New York to broadcast.
In the video, Julissa plays the role of an obnox-
ious "cell phone girl" who bumps into people all
over the city because she's too preoccupied with
her phone conversation. At the end, the video
suggests that a cab is about to run Julissa over.
Julissa became Pines's muse, and he her appre-

ciative Svengali. When someone mentioned what a great body his charge had, he said, "You have no idea. You just have no idea."

Pines is a colorful character who claims to have worked as a "personal technician" for Mick Jagger and other rock stars. He says his autobiography should be called *TV Technician to the Stars*. According to Pines, he and Julissa had a very close relationship. "I became her person and she became my person," he said. "I loved that girl dearly and she loved me."

Like everyone who knew Julissa, Pines was aware that she worshiped Marilyn Monroe, and like all her close friends, he worried that she was channeling her idol's drug and alcohol abuse. But then in April 2007, Julissa had an epiphany. She woke up one day—coincidentally, the exact date was April 14, according to her journal—determined not to continue living the way she had been. *I woke up April 14 and said, "I can't do this anymore,"* she wrote. *I'm turning 24 in two weeks and need to change.*

She swore off drugs and alcohol and joined

Alcoholics Anonymous. "She was going through an amazing period, pulling her life together," Pines said. "I was watching her become a woman."

Julissa's sobriety became the number one issue in her life, and she quit her bartending job because being around liquor for an eight-hour shift was too tempting. She had a tattoo on her ankle of the date her sobriety began. Her mother, Carmen, was overjoyed and told Julissa on Mother's Day 2008 that her daughter being sober was the best gift she could have given her.

And she was serious about her new life. She attended AA meetings daily, resisted friends who asked her to party, and began calling up old buddies like Sarah to make amends. She apologized and told Sarah how much she had changed. She began taking psychology classes at a local college. Her old friend could see some of the changes for herself—she went from bleached blond to brunette, and became a vegetarian.

Sarah told Julissa she was going through a tough time because her baby nephew had died of SIDS (sudden infant death syndrome), and Julissa immediately made a donation to an organization devoted to preventing the syndrome. "She prayed every night for my brother's family," Sarah said.

Julissa focused on school and helping others, and decided she wanted to become a substance abuse counselor because of all the help she'd received from AA. She enrolled in classes at the City College of New York, which is where she met Jack Bennett, coordinator of the school's certified alcohol and substance abuse counselor program. He found her "shy and self-effacing," two adjectives that never would have applied two years earlier. "I think she wanted a better life where she could be proud of who she was and where she was going," Bennett said. Julissa always stood out from the other students because of "the way she was put together from head to toe. [Class is] held on Saturday mornings and a lot of kids come in looking like they just rolled out of bed, but not her. She was always dressed just so.

"She was very young, kind of demure. And one of the things that really impressed me about her was, well, you usually find two types of students," Bennett said. "One is a student that just kind of looks at the professor as the authority on everything and accepts anything and everything I would say. And then there's a student that is very questioning, suspicious. I kind of like those students. I mean, maybe at the time they can be a pain, but these students, they have independent-thinking skills, critical-thinking skills."

That's the category, he said, that Julissa fell into.

This was a whole new phase of Julissa's life, but it was not without some of the tensions from her party-girl past. Even though she was no longer working as a bartender, and had no "regular" job, friends noticed that she was never short of money. She bought her little sister a new computer and dressed herself in designer clothes and accessories. When Prada came out with its new gold and black aviator sunglasses that retail for around $300, she immediately bought a pair, and noted on her Facebook page that she could not wait until the new Chanel glasses came out so she could add those to her collection. She also began traveling all over the United States and beyond. She went to London and Iceland, and in the States visited Washington, D.C., Boston, and Los Angeles. Her boyfriend Tommy, whom she adored, lived in Colorado, as did one of her closest girlfriends.

Julissa was hyper, downing Red Bulls and staying up for hours. Pines, who was working on a play called *The Curse of Beauty*, believed Julissa was plagued by the curse herself. She was always getting hit on, which, Pines said, "can build up your self-esteem but batter your self-worth."

Matthew Terhune, a photographer from Queens, said that Julissa's stories about how she made money and what she was doing when she traveled "never really made a lot of sense. She was kind of vague."

She told Terhune that she could earn as much as $1,000 a night working bachelor parties, even though all she supposedly had to do was walk around in a bikini. "She would say, 'I get paid to look pretty,' " he said. "We said, 'That's all?' But she always said, 'Ooh, I would never touch them. That's gross.' "

Aside from being the hot girl at a party, Julissa was working as a masseuse, one who gave sensual or erotic massages. What is a "sensual" or "erotic" massage? It depends on whom you ask, but Julissa insisted to most of her friends that it was just a massage where she would wear provocative clothing, and perhaps go a little further than a masseuse would at a legitimate spa. She wasn't licensed, but she was serious about it. She had a trained masseuse teach her and she bought her own massage table.

She often placed ads—under various aliases like Morgan, Susie, or Rachel—for her special massages on Craigslist. Her friend Sarah said that Julissa was very clear about what she was doing, and always made sure to include the phrase "no full service" in the ads. "She didn't like to talk about it very much. She didn't do anything outside her boundaries. She never had sex with anybody. It was not prostitution. She did not think highly of prostitution. When she heard someone she knew was going to get into that, she thought it was a horrible idea, and dangerous. She would say, 'I would never have sex for any amount of money.' "

It was the art of sensual massage that brought Julissa to Boston that Monday, April 13. She met a cute Yale medical student on the train. They exchanged phone numbers and spoke of a possible date while she was in Boston. Not long after, Julissa checked into her room at the Marriott hotel in Copley Square.

The day went without incident. Julissa took care of her regulars—the guys who understood what "sensual massage" meant—and then she asked a girlfriend to post an ad on Craigslist under the name Morgan to drum up new business.

That girlfriend later provided ABC News with Julissa's Craigslist ad. The posting was headlined: "Hot Brunette Model & Massuse [sic]—visiting Today." It read:

Hi! My girlfriend Morgan, the massage therapist, will be visiting Boston Monday 4/13 (available from 1pm until 11pm); Tues 4/14 from 7am–11pm; and Wed 4/15 from 7am–12noon checkout!) She visits only once every 1–2 months so don't miss her! Her pics are real, recent, and attached to this message. She is visiting just these couple of days and I highly recommend her! If you would like to schedule, PLEASE E-MAIL back SEVERAL TIME PREFERENCES that work for you during Morgan's window of availability and I will do my best to accommodate you. Be sure to INCLUDE YOUR PHONE NUMBER; I do not give out a contact number until you have provided yours! Kisses XOXO Morgan & Mary.

With the ad posted, Julissa settled into her routine, communicating back and forth by email and phone with Sarah and other friends. She was a nonstop poster on Facebook. It was a quiet night for business. She stayed in her hotel room, as she often did when traveling. Monica says that Julissa was never very curious about the cities she visited, preferring instead to order room service and watch TV. On that night, she ordered a Dane Cook movie and then fell asleep.

4

My 10 P.M. Is Here

On the morning of April 14, 2009, Julissa Brisman woke up in her twentieth-floor room at the Marriott Copley energized and jazzed from the movie she had watched the night before. As she wrote on her Facebook wall: *Almost forgot just how good staying in and watching a funny Dane Cook movie can be.*

At some point in her day, Julissa attended a local meeting of Alcoholics Anonymous.

Friends say she was religious about attending and always sought out meetings even when traveling. In between seeing clients and posting ads on Craiglist for her services, Julissa hung out on Facebook, her virtual playground, and did more emailing with friends. At 4:04 p.m., she posted her favorite bands on her Facebook page. They were, in order, the Killers, Led Zeppelin, Third Eye Blind, the Cure, and Every Avenue. Those were her favorites, but Mark Pines was fascinated at the variety of music she listened to—everyone from Britney Spears to Leonard Cohen.

By 5:03 p.m., she was chatting back and forth on Facebook with Jeramie "Jay" Gray, a guy she'd hung around with in her high school years. Jay said they had lost touch and he'd located her on Facebook only about a month earlier. "She was like a little sister to me," he said.

Since getting back in touch, Jay had been trying to get Julissa, whom he remembered as a party girl, to go out with him and his friends.

She always begged off, as she did that night. She didn't even tell Jay that she was in Boston; he believed she was in New York. Their conversation went back and forth on Facebook:

Julissa: hahah It's not even 5 p.m. and you're out??

Jay: Nah, girl, the parties just started. You don't know I'm Mr. Party all the time?

Julissa: hahah . . . ur fuckeng [sic] crazy!!lol i'm actually tired for the 1st time in like forever i'm not super duper Hyper!!

Jay: whatever the case is. The fact still remains you're about to pass out and I'm about to go out.

Jay chided her about her inability to hang "with the big dogs" and she jokingly shot back that he was an "ass."

There was work to be done. Julissa's girlfriend, the one who had placed the Craigslist ad, had received an email from a guy in Boston. The girlfriend emailed the guy Julissa's cell phone number and let Julissa know he'd be calling. Soon enough, a man with a polite tone told her he was visiting from out of town and would like to see her that night around 10 p.m.

I hope that's not too late for you.

No prob . . . up until 11 p.m. is good.

Five minutes before he was due to show up, Julissa was on the phone with Sarah. Julissa said she had to hang up because of this new client, whom she described as sounding "friendly and cordial." As she had many times before, Sarah told her friend to be careful. "She'd tell me I was a little bit paranoid," Sarah said. "I kind of was like a mother hen."

Sarah insisted that Julissa send her a text when he arrived but on the night of April 14, Sarah's phone was silent.

5

Are You Okay, Buddy?

That April 14, Jill Stern happened to be on the twentieth floor of the Marriott down the hall and across the way from Julissa Brisman's room. Jill was with her seventeen-year-old son Lenny on a springtime college tour. That day they had visited Boston University and crossed it off their list—Lenny didn't like the vibe.

Jill, a forty-nine-year-old dynamo who lives in Greenwich Village, is a successful Realtor and also sells her own jewelry at a small boutique in a hip part of Manhattan. She and her son were in their room that evening sometime after 10 p.m. and Jill was reading a mystery novel, *Manhattan Nocturne* by Colin Harrison, when she heard something down the hall.

"I heard what sounded like a commotion," she said. "It sounded like maybe some furniture was being moved, and then I heard a shriek. I thought, 'What the hell was that?' It was high-pitched and, to my ear, it sounded like a child. I thought maybe a kid was having a fight with her parents or something."

Jill tried to go back to reading her book, but then she heard another shriek. Her son heard it, too. Jill waited a moment and then opened her door. Down the hall, she saw what she thought was a child lying on the hallway carpet, half in and half out of her room. "In my mind, I thought it was a child because that's what the sound was like, and this person was small."

This person, Jill would later find out, was Julissa Brisman. Her dark brown hair was splayed all around her face, her head was down. Jill didn't see anyone else. Still thinking it was some kind of temper tantrum between a child and her parent, Jill called out:

Are you okay, buddy?

There was no answer, and Jill asked her son to take a look. He agreed that whatever was going on did not look good. As Jill thought about calling security, the elevator down the hall opened; a young woman stepped out and began heading in the direction of Julissa, sprawled out on the hallway carpet, and Jill, who was still standing outside her room. The woman stopped immediately when she spotted the body on the carpet. "Holy shit," she said. "She scared the shit out of me." The woman, who appeared a bit tipsy, opened the door to the room right next to the one the body was hanging out of, went inside, and slammed the door shut.

Around this time, Jill says she heard "a guttural sound." All this while, Julissa had not moved nor responded to Jill's continued shouts of concern. She wasn't waiting any longer. "I dialed the operator and told them to come up to the twentieth floor. I couldn't tell them exactly what room but I told them I was in 2041 and this was on the other side, just down the hall." Julissa's room was actually 2034.

"A security guard came up almost immediately and bent down to the woman on the floor. He moved her hair away and I could see blood."

The guard seemed to nearly panic. "Jesus Christ. Jesus Christ," he repeated.

He looked up at Jill.

Get back in your room.

But Jill isn't the type to take orders. She stayed in the hallway. The guard barked into his walkie-talkie.

This is an emergency. Call EMTs and the police right away.

Julissa was alive, but barely. She was dying right there on a nondescript hallway carpet, facedown in her own blood. The guard turned her over and continued talking into his two-way, pleading for someone to help.

As Jill watched, another guard soon joined

the first. He stepped into the room to look around. For the first time, Jill thought about what a close call this had been. If she'd stepped into the hallway when she first heard the commotion, she might have seen Julissa's attacker, but then again, he would have seen her and who knows what would've happened. She shuddered.

Soon the paramedics were on the scene, working on the girl, whom Jill now knew was an adult woman. The hallway filled up with responding police officers and then detectives. Both made a point of interviewing Jill, her son, and anyone else who had a room in the hallway. Since it became apparent that Julissa was shot, the police asked Jill if she'd heard gunshots—but she had not.

But as police officers escorted her past Julissa's room, Jill did see one more thing—the mirrored glass closet just inside the room was shattered, and Jill could see the round impressions left by two bullets.

Julissa had been mortally wounded. She died at 10:36 p.m. in the emergency room at Boston Medical Center.

Thousands of miles away, Sarah, Julissa's close friend, was worried. She had not received the usual text from Julissa signaling that her client had arrived, nor had she received one telling her the client had left. She waited an hour and then called Julissa's hotel room, but no one answered.

Maybe I'm overreacting.

Sarah remembered that Julissa had told her about this cute Yale student she'd met on the train and how they might get together for a date. "I texted her: 'Have fun with your Yale boy . . . just text me when you get a chance, let me know you're okay.' "

Sarah went to sleep, but at 4 a.m. she woke up. She checked her phone but there were no texts from Julissa. She knew immediately that something was wrong. She called the hotel again and asked to speak to security but they would not tell her anything. Finally, one of the guards had a suggestion—call the Boston Police.

Sarah did, and learned that her worst fear had come true: Julissa had been murdered.

6

That's a Good Picture

Once Boston homicide detectives debriefed Jill Stern, examined the crime scene at the Marriott, and learned of the robbery that had occurred only four days earlier at the Westin, they knew that they had a big problem, a problem that had the potential to get a whole lot bigger a whole lot faster. They had little doubt that one man was responsible for both of the hotel attacks. And he was operating in the posh Back Bay. These were not fly-by-night hotels on the outskirts of town; they were in the heart of the most heavily visited part of Boston. What's more, tens of thousands of tourists poised to stay in these very hotels were about to descend on the city for the Boston Marathon. As if that were not enough, two of the sports-crazed city's teams—the Bruins and the Celtics—were in the playoffs, and the Red Sox were beginning their season. If the hotel killer continued his rampage, there was no telling what might happen.

But before they could worry about the future, detectives had to concentrate on the two cases at hand. There were obvious signs that the two crimes were connected. Both women had advertised sensual, if not outright sexual, services on Craigslist. Because of Trisha's previous record for prostitution, detectives had little doubt about what she had been offering at the Westin. They were less sure in the case of Julissa Brisman. All they really knew was that she was offering some type of sensual massage. There was no evidence her killer had received a massage, however; Julissa was still fully clothed when Jill Stern saw her body in the hallway. Based on what Trisha had told them, this appeared to be a robbery gone very wrong when Julissa fought back.

In both cases, the assailant used plastic zip tie restraints—commonly referred to as plastic handcuffs and used by cops making arrests at large demonstrations. Trisha had been subdued with them but escaped quickly once her attacker left her alone. Julissa had one dangling from her wrist, evidence that she had probably fought back while her attacker was trying to get her other hand tied up. It appeared the struggle occurred before her murderer had time to rob her.

The man pulled a gun both times, in Julissa's case using it to deadly effect. He shot her three times at point-blank range. The bullets tore into her ribs, spinal cord, and lung, with the fatal shot going right through her heart. Julissa's head also showed evidence of blunt trauma, and according to her family, detectives believed that her attacker bashed her in the head when she resisted. Clearly, the killer had panicked, because Julissa was found shot to death in the doorway of her room, an extremely risky move because anyone could have seen or heard the attack. Jill Stern said she had not heard any shots but she did hear *something*. The upper half of Julissa's body was on the hallway carpet, the bottom half still inside her room. Jill Stern said the part of Julissa that she could see was fully clothed.

If there was even a tiny doubt about whether the same man was involved in both cases, it was erased when detectives checked out the surveillance photos from the Marriott Copley and the mall attached to the hotel. There at the top of the escalators—a spot familiar to thousands of Bostonians who take the same route every day—was a tall, blond man leaving the scene, and again he was calmly looking at his BlackBerry or phone like he hadn't a care in the world. He didn't even bother to disguise his appearance with a hat.

• • •

The moment detectives saw those photos, their thoughts turned to Trisha Leffler. Where was she, anyway? A person who operated out of the mainstream as Leffler did had no reason to stay in Boston after the robbery. In fact, Trisha said the only reason she had stayed was because the cops still had her cell phone. She had been bugging them to get it back, and they'd promised she could pick it up at ten thirty that morning, but now they were eager to show her the surveillance photographs of the suspect from the Brisman murder.

"The detectives called me and told me not to move, that they would be there soon," she said. "When they came in, one of them handed me a piece of paper with a photograph on it."

Oh this is a really good picture of him. Where did you get it?

Is this the guy who robbed you?

Yeah, how did you get this picture? It's really good. Is this from the same night?

No, we got this last night at the Marriott.

What do you mean?

We believe the same guy who robbed you murdered a girl last night at the Marriott.

"My heart sank," Trisha said. "And then they told me they needed to keep my phone longer and they were putting a rush on [fingerprinting] the tape that was covering my mouth because the guy was not wearing gloves when he taped my mouth."

Later that morning, as forensic investigators were combing Julissa's twentieth-floor hotel room for evidence, a big break came in.

Julissa's heartbroken friend Sarah, upon hearing that her friend had been murdered, was able to locate the email the presumed killer had sent in response to Julissa's Craigslist ad. Sarah wasn't sure, but she thought police could somehow trace the emails back to the man who had sent them, the man she now believes was her friend's killer. She forwarded that email to the Boston detectives.

Paul LaRosa and Maria Cramer

7

The Craigslist Killer

On the morning of April 15, Maria Cramer, a thirty-two-year-old crime reporter at the *Boston Globe*, was at home when an editor called her cell phone. "He told me there was a report of a woman shot at the Copley Marriott in Boston."

Cramer felt the rush of adrenaline kick in. She knew this wasn't your average homicide. "The Copley Marriott is a very elegant Back Bay hotel. And so hearing that a woman had been shot like this in a hotel room, I knew immediately it was going to be a big story," she said. "We heard that she was possibly involved in some sort of escort service. Then the news began changing. Maybe she was involved in some sort of erotic services. And as the story unfolded, we learned that she had advertised on Craigslist as a masseuse who was coming to Boston to provide massages to, you know, whoever wanted them. Later on that day we learned that police were looking at how this was connected to a robbery that had taken place [less than] a week earlier. And this was a robbery of a prostitute from Las Vegas. The robbery had taken place right across from the hotel where the killing had taken place. This is at the Westin."

Cramer began calling every name she had compiled in the two years she'd been covering the crime beat for the paper. "You start calling everybody you know, anybody who can help you. Anybody that you know works in a certain district. Anybody that you know works in a certain division. Any office," she said. "You contact the prosecutor's office, the police department. You contact the public information officer. The people who aren't issuing public information but you know are on the ground. You really need to work the phones as far as finding victim's friends, relatives. You look for anybody who will talk to you about who this person was."

The story broke at what was a very sensitive time for the *Globe*. The management team of *The New York Times*, the *Globe*'s parent company, had threatened to close the newspaper permanently on May 1 if it did not win substantial cuts from the *Globe*'s unions. The deadline was approaching, the negotiations were ongoing, and for Cramer, this big murder story could not have come at a better time. At least now her mind was occupied by something other than the union negotiations and the anxiety of knowing that she and everyone else at the *Globe* could very well lose their jobs.

Cramer's sources soon gave her the outlines

of the story, mentioning the coincidence of the plastic zip ties and the fact that both women had advertised on Craigslist. *That* caught everyone's attention. So many people use Craigslist and feel so comfortable with it that it was upsetting to hear that a killer was using it to pick out victims like the rest of us might pick out a used kitchen table. At the same time, the story fueled criticism that the Internet is a dangerous place, full of bad people. This fed people's fears in a very real way, and it was certainly possible that the killer was out there looking for more victims. "It basically created a frenzy not only in the media but from the police because of the way the two cases were connected," Cramer recounted. "You had the possibility of a serial criminal here."

And this story—which would eventually be dubbed the "Craigslist Killer" case—was very much Internet related, in more ways than just Craigslist. In the days before the Internet, when a story like this broke, a reporter would go to the home, school, and workplace of those involved, and buttonhole anyone coming and going. Another reporter back in the newsroom would grab a reverse directory, look up the victim's address, and begin calling all his or her neighbors to glean what he could. All of that still takes place, but these days, the *first* place a reporter is likely to turn to in a story like this is Facebook, the social networking site that's become as ubiquitous to our lives as Craigslist. And Facebook has made every reporter's job much easier. Almost every young person, Julissa included, has a Facebook page under his or her real name, and unless the person sets everything to private, which few people do, anyone can look up a person's friends—often by category. Want to know who the person went to high school or college with, or who she works with? That's easy. Immediately, a reporter has the names and email addresses of those closest to the victim—not just the people who live in her building. From there, it is often simple to track people's phone numbers and home addresses. Facebook is a reporter's best friend.

It's a tool that Cramer was not shy about utilizing. "Everybody has a Facebook page. We looked up all the friends and started calling everybody who was her friend. And that's really how we were able to break a lot of the stuff," she said. "We happened to hit the right people. But the only way to do that is by calling and calling and calling. And it's exhausting."

In a lot of cases, the police do not readily release surveillance photos but, in this case, with the killer on the loose, they were happy to. The grainy image from the Westin and the much better pictures from the Marriott were soon aired by television stations all across New England, and then the country by an eager press who smelled a hot story. When Cramer and her editors looked at the photos, they could not help but notice the demeanor of the tall blond man at the center of the case. "One of the things that we were struck by was how casual he looked," she said. "How nonchalant he looked as he was coming down the [escalator], as he was looking at his BlackBerry. He looked like somebody who had just stepped out of the hotel bar where he'd been watching a game and downing a beer. He didn't look like somebody who had committed murder or bound a woman and gagged her and robbed her."

Not only did the apparent killer have a certain "devil may care" attitude but also he was in appearance unlike most murder suspects. He was tall and blond and dressed like he had stepped out of an Abercrombie & Fitch fashion shoot. He looked *familiar*—like any of the tens of thousands of college students in Boston. This guy was a yuppie, complete with BlackBerry. The press—every bit as guilty of lookism as the rest of society—ate it up.

Behind the scenes, Boston detectives were unimpressed. The killer may have been good-looking, well dressed, and carrying a BlackBerry, but he was no criminal mastermind. He had made a ton of rookie mistakes. He had taken off his gloves before touching the black tape he put over Trisha Leffler's mouth, he had

not worn a disguise, and he had used his Black-
Berry and the Internet, two modern accessories
that are an investigator's best friend. Black-
Berrys can be traced to cell phone towers to
pinpoint someone's location. That would be
important once they had a cell phone to trace.
But right now they had something even more
important—the killer's emails, thanks to Julissa's friend Sarah.

8

Digital Forensics

The emails sent to Julissa by the killer were a tremendous lead, almost like having the fingerprints of the murderer. With those emails in hand, forensic investigators—with help from the New York City Police Department's Cyber Crime Unit—set about tracing the killer's IP, or Internet protocol, address. While it sounds high-tech, tracking IP addresses has become an almost routine part of police work in the twenty-first century.

"There's a lot of gumshoe detective work that needs to be done in the electronic world just like in the real world," said Joe Caruso, CEO of Global Digital Forensics, a private consulting firm.

While Caruso did not directly work on the Craigslist case, he is familiar with it and has served as an expert witness in many high-profile cases. Caruso said the killer's carelessness with his IP address was the equivalent of leaving digital bread crumbs from the hotels back to his home. He might as well have left his wallet at the scene.

What most people do not realize is that every computer—once it connects to the Internet—receives a distinct IP address from the computer user's Internet service provider. It makes only a slight difference if that connection comes by cable or phone line. Cable companies generally keep their IP addresses static while phone companies change them frequently, but it doesn't matter—phone companies always know who has which IP address.

And that electronic address is as unique as a person's phone number. No two are exactly alike, and once the police have a person's IP address, it is usually only a matter of time before they can trace that IP address to the person's home address.

There are exceptions to the rule. Had the Craigslist Killer been more sophisticated, he would have disguised his IP address by using what is called a proxy server, a routing service that can make it seem like you are sitting in Hong Kong when in fact you're in Brooklyn. Proxy servers are readily available on the Internet. Or the killer could have made his "dates" while logged on from a public wireless setting, like a Starbucks or an Internet café. But he took neither of those precautions. He made the mistake many people do, thinking that the Internet makes one anonymous when the truth is you're anything but. It later came out that the killer had created a new email account before contacting Julissa's friend, but it didn't matter—his IP address remained the same.

"Privacy on the Internet is a complete illusion," said Paul Parisi, chief technology officer of a company called DNSstuff.com in Newburyport, Massachusetts.

DNSstuff.com's highly sophisticated web tools are used by the FBI, the Secret Service, Interpol, and any number of police organizations around the world. Parisi said he knows by monitoring his company's website and by "verbal confirmation" that police investigators used DNSstuff.com's software to track down the IP address from the Craigslist Killer's email.

When you receive an email, typically the IP address of the sender is hidden from view, but most times, it is still there. It's contained in the "header" of the message, which is like a boarding pass complete with departure and arrival data, any connecting flights (other computers it passes through), and the date and time. It can be accessed differently in various email programs but often just by going into the "mail preferences" part of the message. The header information is critical for the routing of the email but it's generally irrelevant to the people reading the contents of the email.

In this case, the killer is believed to have used an email account originating from Yahoo! That was another critical mistake. He would have had much more cover if he'd used an email program like Google's Gmail, which omits the sender's IP address from the header. By using Yahoo!, the killer's originating computer's IP address was right there for the police to read. It was akin to a smoking gun. "He was swinging in the wind at that point," Caruso said, "because he didn't make any real effort to conceal his Internet ID."

Of course, the killer surely did not know—as most people do not—that Gmail is a much better place from which to send email if you're thinking of engaging in criminal activity. Yahoo! and Hotmail are not nearly as discreet because one's IP address is always included.

Tracking an IP address is so straightforward and easy that you can do it yourself—just by going to Whatismyipaddress.com. There is even a button on that site that says *IP Lookup*. Click it, and not only will it show the name of your cable or DSL provider but also your exact physical location within a few neighborhoods. Of course, the Boston PD needed to have more information than the general neighborhood where the killer lived. Knowing the Internet service provider meant police could subpoena or simply ask the ISP to look up the subscriber name attached to that IP address on that specific date. An investigator could scarcely ask for anything more.

And the investigators in this case were not relying solely on IP addresses. Remember that Trisha Leffler told police her attacker made a point of erasing his phone number from her cell phone. That might seem clever, but in truth, it is hopelessly naive. The attacker's cell phone number would still have been present on the running table of phone numbers kept by Trisha's cell phone provider. All police had to do, again, was either contact or subpoena Trisha's cell phone provider and obtain a list of phone calls made to her cell phone late on

April 9 and early on April 10. With that information in hand, they could cross-check the name attached to that number against the one that turned up with the IP address. If the names matched, that meant the same man was almost definitely involved in both attacks, and at that point, the cops would be on very solid ground. The exception would be if the attacker had obtained a disposable phone from a company that does not require the buyer to provide any information.

And the police would have yet another avenue available to them once they knew the killer's cell phone number and service provider. Nearly every cell phone now comes with a built-in GPS (global positioning system) chip, so every cell phone can be tracked. It requires no special program. All cell phones are continually communicating with or "pinging" nearby cell towers, whether or not they are in use. In fact, this pinging is going on even when your phone is turned off. The *only* way to prevent a phone from being tracked is to remove the battery. (But even that can be used against you in court, as it was used against convicted murderer and computer genius Hans Reiser in Oakland in 2008. In that case, when police located Reiser's missing wife's cell phone in her car, the battery had been removed. When they picked up Reiser for questioning, the battery had been taken out of his cell phone as well. The district attorney called the removal of the batteries "a signature" of the killer, just one of many pieces of evidence against Reiser.)

The constant communication between your cell phone and nearby cell towers is done to make sure you get the best coverage. It's how your phone knows how many bars of service it has. As you travel around, your phone is always searching for the best signal strength and often communicating with two or more towers at a time. Because of all this, there is a record of where your cell phone is—where *you* are—at all times. Since the killer can be seen in the surveillance photos using his BlackBerry, the police assumed it was turned on, and once they obtained his cell phone records, they suspected they would be able to track his movements through his cell phone and compare the places he had been with the times and locations of the crimes.

"You take the surveillance video from the hotel, the cell phone calls, the emails, the location data, you put it all together and [the Boston police] have a very compelling case," said Caruso.

He's right. By using the relatively new science of digital forensics, the police could make a pretty strong case against Julissa's murderer— even without any other physical evidence. Clearly, Julissa's killer did not stop to consider any of this.

"I don't think he was as technically adept as he put himself out there to be," said Caruso. "I call it 'cyber stupidity.' "

9

Julissa's Secrets

While the police worked their angles, print reporters and television producers from every media outlet in the country were working theirs. Julissa's friends on Facebook were simple to track down, and since many of them had not even heard about her death in those first few hours, they were eager to call reporters back.

"I'm always amazed that somebody wants to talk to me about the person that they lost,"

Maria Cramer said. "I'm always amazed by how strong people are. And when they're willing to talk about their loved one and share that story with me, I'm so grateful. I think that's part of what I love about doing the crime beat. It's that you meet these incredible people."

Julissa's friend Jay Gray woke up on April 15 to a voice mail from a *New York Times* reporter. He had no idea why the guy would be calling him, but he called back and learned that his good friend Julissa had been shot to death. "I didn't know what to think," Jay said. "I mean, I could not put it together."

Mark Pines got the news directly from Julissa's mother at around 7 a.m. the morning after the murder. "My phone rang and I was still pretty groggy," he said, according to an interview he did with Momlogic, a parenting blog. "Carmen, Julissa's mother, called me. She paused for a second and said, 'Julissa died.' I knew there was no going back after that statement. We cried over the phone together for twenty minutes. I couldn't even ask her what happened. She said she had to go to Boston."

Pines soon found out. "At nine a.m., my phone started ringing," he said. "The news agencies started calling me. I knew something happened and Googled her name.

"At this point, the surveillance photos were turning up. The photos showed the alleged perpetrator texting on the way up and on the way down. She was not naive, and she knew how to screen people. She never made an appointment on the first call, and she had a good screening process. He got by her."

Sarah and other friends said they had warned Julissa to be careful, but at the same time, they were not at all surprised that she resisted being robbed. It's very possible that the killer's disarming appearance may have had something to do with that. Julissa had been raised on the tough streets of upper Manhattan and Hell's Kitchen, and being robbed by a tall, blond, *preppy* guy must have seemed on some level like a joke, maybe even an insult. There's a chance that Julissa, who considered herself street-smart, did not take her attacker seriously until it was too late. Then again, she probably would have resisted *any* robber, at least according to Monica, a very close friend.

"Fighting back was totally a part of her character," Monica said. "She was a tough and sometimes scandalous girl. She was sweet, but if anything bit her, she would go crazy! Trust me, if she was mugged on a Manhattan street, she would not have given up her purse for anything, and she could have died stabbed by a mugger instead. I actually think that if she had given the guy her money, he wouldn't have killed her, but she fought and screamed and the guy probably got nervous and killed her. I also warned her, I told her to be smart, that the money is just not worth it and if anything should happen, to just give it up and stay quiet. She would answer jokingly that [she would] kick their asses."

With the killer still roaming free, and Trisha Leffler hiding out, Julissa became the focus of the story. Everyone wanted to know exactly what type of services she was offering in that

Boston hotel room, and why she had put herself in such a vulnerable position. It was a "blame the victim" mentality at its worst because, at least on the surface, it appeared that sex had nothing to do with her murder. The guy was after money, end of story. But to a lot of people—who broadcast their feelings on blogs far and wide—Julissa was nothing more than a prostitute and would never have been such an easy target if she had not been engaging in a risqué and risky business.

Julissa's friends fought back against the innuendo and gossip, insisting that their friend was not a prostitute. They did, however, grudgingly admit that, yes, she was playing with fire. They knew it; she knew it. After all, it's one thing to set the boundaries of "sensual" massage as you understand it, but who informs the clients or tells them what they're getting? The sex trade operates on innuendo and enticement—not step-by-step instructions. "I told her to get her act together," Monica said. "I warned her so many times."

But as strippers and prostitutes often discover, the money in the sex trade is often too good to up and quit, especially when the alternative is to make $400 or $500 a week instead of $1,000 a day. Kristin Davis should know. The flamboyant former madam was arrested for running a call-girl ring in New York, and she says the money can be hard to turn down, especially once you get used to it. "If you come from working at a restaurant, you're making a couple hundred dollars a shift, maybe," Davis said. "And all of a sudden, you're making thousands of dollars a week. Once you've adjusted your lifestyle, it's hard to readjust . . . to a normal level. Their whole vision of what reality is is skewed."

When she was in business, Davis said she posted some three hundred ads a day on Craigslist at $5 a pop. Some of those were for Julissa, who, Davis said, was working for her. "She's a very pretty girl. She came to me as a blond. She looked great as a blond," Davis said. "Then she dyed her hair dark. She looked great as a brunette. She took very good care of herself."

And Julissa's clients noticed. Davis said Julissa had a stable of regular clients. Davis agrees that, as everyone says, Julissa's specialty was erotic massage: "She did body rub. And body rub is characterized by a pretty girl in lingerie giving a sensual massage. Escorting is completely different, so in terms of working for me, she only did body rub. Some touching involved, but no sex."

Davis last heard from Julissa about a month before she was murdered when she actually checked in with Davis to see how the madam was holding up after her arrest. "She was dating someone, she was happy," Davis said. "She was working for herself. She conveyed that she missed me and was upset for what happened to me, which was, you know, a really nice thing to hear from her."

Monica said she tried to warn Julissa away from her body rub business but her friend would not listen. "I always told her to get a real

job or study something. I told her to be careful
with the job and the clients but she assured me
that she was only seeing the regulars and it was
fine," Monica said. "She always claimed to be a
tough Manhattan girl who could take care of
herself. I know she loved the money and would
go on eight-hundred-dollar daily shopping
sprees to Chanel or Gucci. She would tell me
the strangest stories about the guys, calling
them creeps, but I know deep inside it was all
about the easy money. I don't think she would
have stopped anytime soon."

Another friend admitted that Julissa had
told her that she sometimes pranced around
those "special" parties—for which she was paid
so much money—topless. But her main business was massage. "She thought of it as a mod-
eling gig," her former roommate said. "I think
she was feeling like she was doing a massage
but being paid more because she was a model."

Monica says Julissa once tried to talk her
into giving it a try when Monica was complain-
ing about all the bills she had from school. "She

tried to convince me to do this to pay for my studies, that's why I know all the details," she said. "She said it was good and easy, but that's not me, and although I could understand and maybe would have loved to live the Gucci life, it's not me."

Monica says Julissa did *not* provide full service—intercourse—but she did help her male clients climax at the end of the massage. That's the polite way of phrasing it. To be impolite, she gave her clients a hand job, or least that's what Monica says Julissa told *her*. "Sensual massage consists of a one-hour massage with a happy ending, and the girl is in very provocative clothes. The man can't touch, and there is no other sexual activity. Just a laid-back and relaxed happy ending. The clients were normally regulars—rich lawyers and doctors. Sometimes, when the day was slow, she'd put an ad up to get some newcomers. Her business extended nationwide. Many times she would leave for two or three weeks at a time, going from coast to coast, city to city, spending as much as two to three days in one place. She could see up to eight clients a day, making up to a thousand dollars a day."

Monica claims that some of Julissa's trips to other cities and abroad were organized by a mysterious man who put together a stable of beauties, arranged the travel, and then split the girls' tips. Monica said she tried to get the guy busted without success. She believes, however, that Julissa was moving away from her "benefactor" and, on the night she was killed, was most likely working for herself.

By 11 a.m. on April 15, Julissa's mother, Carmen, and other members of her family were meeting with the police in Boston. She told them what she could about her daughter and then made the painful identification of the deceased.

Down in New York, there was one other woman very worried about the Craigslist Killer. Jill Stern had spoken to the press the day after the murder. Her photo and last name, along with the handy information that she lived in Greenwich Village, were there for anyone to see, including the killer.

"I'm very easy to track down on the Internet," she said. "Once you have my name, you can find my photo, where I live, where I sell jewelry. It's all there."

What's more, her Village condo is on the first floor, and at least one reporter walked right past the doorman and knocked on her door. The fact that the killer was still at large and could do the same thing was freaking Jill out—she changed her locks, not only on her apartment but also on her summer house out on Long Island.

10

On the Trail of a Killer

*I*f you passed by the Marriott Hotel near Copley Square on Thursday, April 16, you would have seen camera crews trained on the front door as if the killer was going to barge through at any moment. In truth, the television reporters were talking to their viewers and colleagues back in the studios, who were relaying the scandalous story to the rest of the country.

The Craigslist Killer story had become *the* number one topic of conversation in Boston. It wasn't so much that Bostonians were afraid—the killer clearly had targeted young women involved in the sex trade who were advertising on Craigslist—but the robbery and murder in one of the best areas of Boston had captured everyone's imagination. The city was getting ready for the Boston Marathon, and the posh Back Bay went on with business as usual. Office workers bustled down Huntington Avenue. Jocks preparing for the marathon took off for light runs down the Esplanade. Tourists headed for nearby Newbury Street, a strip of lovely upscale restaurants and designer boutiques like Valentino, Max Mara, and Cartier.

And behind the scenes, investigators were working nonstop. In the middle of this maelstrom was Sergeant Detective Daniel Duff, a twenty-year veteran of the Boston PD who had worked in homicide for the past three years and was the on-call detective the night of Julissa's murder. It would be up to him and the two detectives he supervises, Jimmy Freeman and Bobby Kenney, to find the Craigslist Killer.

Tall, with wire-rimmed glasses and thinning salt-and- pepper hair, Duff is soft-spoken, speaks deliberately, and looks more like a college professor than a cop. His boss and friend, Lieutenant Detective Robert Merner, has more of that classic "cop" look. His head is shaved clean, his voice is deep and gravelly with a trace of a Boston accent. The head of the homicide unit, he has a powerful build and an intense laser focus in his eyes when he looks at you that would intimidate Vic Mackey, the detective Michael Chiklis played in the FX series *The Shield*.

On April 15, Merner, Duff, and Duff's men began working the case so intently that they barely slept for the next week. Merner remembers catching at most two or three hours' of sleep a night. When he had time, he would go home and change his shirt or hit the gym. When he was tired, he sat, put his feet up on a chair, and closed his eyes for a few minutes. There was a lot of pressure to solve the case, so much so that detectives barely took the time to eat. "At one point, we went thirty-six hours and all we had in us was coffee," Merner said. "We were ready to kill each other."

They essentially lived at Boston Police headquarters, poring over the surveillance footage to see if there was anything they'd missed. They also sifted through tips to the department's anonymous text tip line—there were more than 170, and each one needed to be checked. Some of the tips were predictable. As always in these types of cases, there were plenty of women sure their ex-boyfriends or husbands were the killer. Other tips were too vague, too devoid of any solid information even to follow. Some were bizarre. "We had a guy that called, for instance," Merner recalled. "Said I'm seventy-one years old, I'm in Florida. I'm a registered sex offender . . . I'm not sure it wasn't me who did it." Merner smiled—even that tip had to go on the record. "Still has to be documented, to be secured," he said.

But the one tip they took seriously was the

one that came from Sarah, Julissa's good friend and former roommate. They felt that if they could track her 10 p.m. client's IP address, they would be on the right track. "The momentum brought us to the point where we couldn't really stop what we were doing, so we just had to continue working," he said.

And they had help. Dozens of cops worked the case from four different department agencies: the Boston Regional Intelligence Center—the division charged with collecting and analyzing tips and other investigative leads—the fugitive squad, special investigations, and the homicide squad. Merner also enlisted the help of the FBI and the New York City police, which has a special Cyber Crime squad, which aided in tracking down the email's IP address.

And while all of this was going on, the killer was not slowing down, not even for a day.

11

On the Move

Jamie, a young mother from Cape Cod, was visiting Foxwoods Resort Casino in Connecticut on Thursday, April 16, along with a male friend. He was playing blackjack, and Jamie was only watching. They were having a great time. The table was rocking and full of fun. The players were joking, carrying on, and then . . . a tall, blond man who was clean-cut and looked to be in his twenties, sat down. Immediately, Jamie felt a chill, almost like he had a black cloud over his head. There was something very dark about this guy.

"Immediately, he gave off a weird energy," Jamie said. "He had a stone-cold face, and he kept looking at me. He was just very, very weird and creepy and he made me very uncomfortable. He was constantly looking at me out of the corner of his eye in a strange way."

Jamie tried not to look back but she could not shake the guy's strange vibe. She watched as he lost one hand after another. "The whole time, he was looking at my chest, looking me up and down. I was so uncomfortable that I sat back and put my purse in front of my chest. He kept throwing down money and he wasn't winning. It was amazing to me. He threw down about six hundred dollars in an hour and a half, and he was losing and rolling his eyes. He was constantly looking at me and I felt so uncomfortable that I told my friend I was going to play the slots. When I went back [to the blackjack table] he was still looking at me and it was very creepy. He was staring in a very intense, strange way.

"On the car ride home, we talked about how bizarre he was and how uncomfortable he made me feel. He played for two and a half hours, and then he got up and mumbled something under his breath, like a curse.

"I called my sister and told her, 'No way on God's green earth would I have sat at that table with another girl.' My friend was a pretty big guy, that's the only reason I stayed . . . that guy had a very blank, evil face."

Later that night, Amber, a twenty-six-year-old exotic dancer from Las Vegas, settled into her room on the third floor of the Holiday Inn Express on Jefferson Boulevard in Warwick, Rhode Island. She did the same thing Trisha and Julissa had done in Boston—she placed an ad on Craigslist. Amber's specialty was the lap dance. She was on the strip club circuit, visiting nightclubs always hungry for hot new talent, and she was in Rhode Island specifically to dance at the Cadillac Lounge in Providence. On the side, she decided to make the most of her free time by doing private and profitable lap dances in her room. The Holiday Inn in Warwick is midway between Foxwoods casino and Boston, off Interstate 95, the perfect spot to stop if you were driving back home after a night of gambling. And if you'd lost money, well, pulling a robbery using a tried-and-true method made sense.

Amber knew none of this. All she knew was that some horny guy wanted to come by her room around eleven o'clock. They agreed on a price—$100 for a lap dance—and Amber said nothing was discussed beyond that. On his way there, he called and texted her. As far as Amber could tell, he was serious about showing up, and he did. At precisely 10:51 p.m., the hotel's surveillance cameras picked up a tall blond man, this time wearing a cap, arriving in the hotel lobby.

By the time the guy reached Amber's room, he was no longer wearing a hat. She said he looked pretty "average." He was young, tall, and blond and was wearing a black jacket, a pink shirt, and blue jeans. They talked for a minute, and Amber noticed that he had an accent.

You're not from around here?

No, I'm from Boston.

"I turned around and he pulled out a gun," Amber said. "His hand was shaking pretty bad. I was scared but I listened to what he said to do."

Amber said it was at that point that the gunman said something that he continued to say about five times during the robbery: "I don't want to kill you. I'm broke and I just need some cash or some cards."

"I was crying a little bit, but I was doing it quietly because I knew he could go off, so I just tried to be quiet."

The gunman had Amber lie facedown on the floor. He tied her hands behind her back with what she later learned were zip ties, the same type used in the two Boston cases. Then he attempted to put a ball gag in her mouth, the sort normally associated with S&M activities. Amber kept shaking her head and the gunman relented. He spotted a computer cord in her room and asked her if she had a computer.

No.

I will kill you right now if I find there's a computer in here.

"I told him there was no computer and right about then my phone started ringing," Amber said later.

That got the gunman extremely nervous.

Who's calling your phone? Why are they calling you?

Amber did not answer but she knew it was her husband. He was traveling with her and he was downstairs in the lobby, waiting for a text from her that the client had arrived in the room. When it didn't arrive, Amber's husband began calling.

The next thing Amber knew, her husband, who had a key, burst into the room. The gunman threatened him with the gun, and her husband turned and ran into the hall. The gunman also ran out of the room, but in the opposite direction. "I jumped up and hit the door with my elbow," Amber said.

Soon enough, her husband returned. The gunman had not taken anything but Amber was very shaken up. "I wasn't crying," she said. "I was in shock."

This time, the getaway was much trickier for the tall blond man—the Warwick Holiday Inn is not in the middle of a city, and he could not simply walk out of the hotel and get lost down a side street or on the T, the Boston subway system. He had to run down three flights of stairs, get in his car, and drive out of the parking lot, but somehow he managed. No one got a look at the car.

The couple went down to the lobby to report what had happened. The zip ties were still on Amber, and a hotel guard had to cut them off. In minutes the police arrived and she told them her story. The one thing she remembered most was the phrase the gunman kept repeating over and over: "I don't want to kill you. I'm broke and I just need some cash or some cards."

The local cops had let the Boston detectives know that they either had a copycat or the now infamous Craigslist Killer had struck again. There was only one way to find out—the cops pulled the hotel's surveillance videos, and sure enough, there he was again, the now familiar figure. Not only had the cameras caught him in the lobby when he arrived but they had also captured his image as he fled down a staircase. When Chief McCarthy later briefed the press on what had happened, he noted that in Rhode Island prostitution is allowed behind closed doors. It is a crime only if a customer flags down a streetwalker.

In the *Globe* newsroom, Cramer was shocked by the brazenness of the criminal. Could the Craigslist Killer really have struck again? And so close to Boston, where everyone was looking for him?

Cramer had a sinking feeling that the crimes were indeed connected. While there were some differences, there were too many similarities—same MO, same website. It had to be him. There was now a serial criminal on the loose, and the biggest fear was whether he'd kill again before police got him.

Detective Duff and his men were incredulous. It was clear something was driving the Craigslist Killer. He was in a frenzy, acting in apparent disregard for his own safety, and seemingly driven by an unseen force to rob people despite all the heat generated by local and national headlines. Investigators wondered if he might be on drugs and needed the money for a fix, or if he was just a sociopath driven by a need to control and subvert women. They knew one thing—he needed to be stopped before someone else got killed.

12

Number 8 Highpoint Circle

For three days, police forensic investigators had been working to trace the killer's email address, and on the night of Saturday, April 18, they received a name and physical address with the help of Comcast, the Internet provider the killer had used to send the telltale email to Julissa's friend. The address sent cops to number 8 Highpoint Circle in Quincy, a neighboring working-class city south of Boston. It was dark outside as at least six police cars, all unmarked, slid into place, moving stealthily as sharks to ensure their target was surrounded. And there they sat, staring at the entrance of the building, a mere ten miles south of Boston.

The killer's email, sent on an account opened only the day before Julissa was murdered, belonged to someone in the building named Philip Markoff. It was an incredible lead—the equivalent of a treasure map marked with an X. But there was still work to be done. The big question: Did Philip Markoff look anything like the man in the hotel stills? One of the cops joked that if this Markoff guy was 5 feet 2 inches and Asian, they would have a problem. There was always a possibility that Markoff's computer had been used by someone else—a neighbor, a friend, someone with access to the apartment—or it could have been taken over by a remote operator sitting miles from this location. If Markoff used a wireless modem and didn't secure it, someone nearby could have accessed his IP address. Investigators were hopeful, but aware that the Highpoint lead might fizzle out, like dozens of others had. The only thing they knew for sure was that they had to eyeball their guy.

It was time to resort to old-fashioned police work, and that meant sitting on the location until they spotted someone who looked like the tall blond man now familiar to every cop working the case.

The Highpoint Circle condominiums are relatively new and somewhat out of step with the rest of Quincy, a blue-collar suburb of Boston whose main street is dotted with stores like Don's Joke Shop and Gentle Dental. The Highpoint Circle complex is something altogether different. It sits on a slight hill and may be *in* Quincy, but it is not *of* Quincy. It affects a certain exclusive air—warranted or not—and the development's management boasts of amenities like a pool room and tennis courts.

It was here that the Boston PD's elite fugitive unit set up shop. To help make the face-to-face identification, the homicide investigators had sent to the scene an esteemed colleague—Sergeant Detective Brian Albert, head of the department's Fugitive Unit. Albert had developed a specialty over the years of being able to match a suspect to surveillance photos, and he had a real eye for picking out telltale details. He was so good that he'd been involved with the capture of nearly every high-profile fugitive nabbed by the Boston PD over the last eight years. Albert, forty, is a former U.S. Marine who honed his skill while serving as an infantry machine gunner in Kuwait City during the first Gulf War. In that position, he was forced to watch every movement of every person who walked nearby. There was often only a split second to decide if the movement was friendly or not.

When he returned to Boston and joined the police department in 1994, he was assigned to the district covering Mattapan and North Dorchester, two of the toughest neighborhoods in the city. Again, he had to watch people's body language, and that skill increased even more when he was transferred to the gang unit where he worked for eight years. "The role of the gang unit is proactive policing," Albert said. "You're trying to suppress gang and gun violence in the city, and that includes getting out of the cars, talking to people on the street. You have to be aware of your surroundings, the action, the movements that people are making."

Then, in 2007, the Boston PD created the Fugitive Unit and put Albert in charge. He was perfect because he was patient, having spent untold hours watching gang members come and go. The Fugitive Unit is more of the same, trying to pick up those who had a vested interest in avoiding cops and being on guard. "You can sit on something for a whole day, two days, a week and never really see what you want to see," he said. "Surveillance is very tough. For every time you think they don't see you, they ultimately see you. They probably pick up on the fact that someone is out there. If you're doing surveillance, it's on someone who has a long criminal history. Their head is on a swivel, just like ours, so they're looking around all the time."

That was not the case with this suspect, Philip Markoff. The entrance of number 8 Highpoint Circle faces a parking lot, and a garage is adjacent, making it very easy for the cops to keep an eye out for anyone coming or going. Since you could not walk anywhere from the development, any resident was sure to be heading for the lot or the garage. You could always leave the lobby from the opposite door, but unless you were visiting the management office or a friend, you were unlikely to go that way.

In any case, Albert's men covered both sides of the building. Nothing much happened Saturday night or into those early morning hours of Sunday, April 19. Stakeouts are always the same—long periods of boredom, and a sudden burst of adrenaline when the target appears. The thing is, you have to stay alert because you never know when something will happen. The unit passed the time listening to music, making phone calls, reading the file on this guy Markoff, and drinking Red Bull. They also switched cars from time to time so there never was the same color car parked near the entrance. People tend to unconsciously notice those visual clues, Albert said.

The officers watched through binoculars with intense focus. "I have a strong mind," Albert said. "I think about things. I think about what we're going to do. I go over scenarios in my head. What if we have to chase him on foot? As the boss, I have to think a little bit more about what we're going to do. They're looking at me for that."

It was slow going until midmorning Sunday when the cops spotted a tall blond man exit the building. An attractive blonde woman was at his side. Investigators perked up. Was this Markoff? Did he match the surveillance videos? Did he have the same type of hair? The right physique? The same gait? He towered over the woman he was with, and that gave them a good sense of his height. He appeared to be over six feet, which checked out. His hair was blond—another check mark. When he walked, he was both awkward and athletic looking. Albert said the way the man carried himself brought to mind Kevin McHale, the great center of the Boston Celtics. "I was surprised at how much he looked like the pictures I saw from the incidents in Boston and Rhode Island," Albert later told the *Boston Herald*. "It was exciting to see him up close."

Duff, too, thought they were onto something. "Everything we had up until that point was, yeah, he looks like the guy," Duff said. "We didn't want to jump to any conclusions, and so we couldn't just go down there and lock him up based on, yes, he's six feet three inches and blond."

Investigators watched as the couple got into a Toyota Corolla, and began tailing them. There was nothing special in what the couple was doing that Sunday. They made a trip to a local BJ's Wholesale Club, where they picked up a case of bottled water and other provisions.

Every aisle they walked down, undercover cops were close by, and they began to pick up on an unusual dynamic between the two. The woman was lovey-dovey, kissing and hugging the man, but he was removed and appeared cold to her. It might have meant nothing, but Albert thought the guy looked "stressed." He was not smiling, and if one can read into these things, as cops do, the man seemed to have a lot on his mind.

"He probably never saw us at all," Albert said. "That was obviously a plus for us because we weren't dealing with someone who is normally looking around all the time or has a long history of selling drugs."

Investigators sent word back to Boston Police headquarters—they thought they had their man. The astute Albert sent out his short but sweet assessment: *I like him*. Given his track record, Albert's word was gold. Other investigators had begun to compile background information on Markoff and they knew he was a twenty-three-year-old graduate student originally from a small town in upstate New York. The woman was his fiancée, Megan McAllister, twenty-five.

Police Commissioner Ed Davis, who had been getting regular reports on the progress of the stakeout, decided to visit the scene himself. At one point, in addition to the Boston Police commissioner, there were at least twenty cops and investigators surrounding number 8 Highpoint Circle. The office of Suffolk district attorney Dan Conley was also closely involved. If an arrest was made, everyone wanted to make sure it went according to the strictest interpretation of the law, so there could be nothing for a defense lawyer to challenge later on.

The rest of that Sunday, Markoff and his fiancée didn't do much of anything, except for the couple of times he came out to tinker under the hood of a second car the couple used.

Megan came out to be at his side. Again, she was bubbly and energetic; he was not. "Giggly," is how one officer described her as she flirted with Markoff while he just looked down at the car's engine. "She looked like she was living in a fairy tale," the cop said.

Sunday lapsed into Monday, April 20, and everyone was getting antsy. Investigators wanted to bring Markoff in for questioning. The cops felt confident they had enough to get a search warrant for his apartment. Those in charge, including lawyers in the office of the DA, wanted one more thing before giving the go-ahead to pick him up—they wanted an eyewitness identification. The word went out again for Trisha Leffler. Where was she now? Fortunately, the twenty-nine-year-old Las Vegas resident was nearby in New York City. She had become an important and critical part of this massive police operation.

"On Monday I got a call from the ADA [assistant district attorney], and she asked me where I was, and I told her I was in New York," Trisha said. "She said, 'We have some photos we'd like to show you. I'm going to have a detective call you.' "

Trisha's phone rang almost immediately. It

was one of the investigators. "He said they had a couple of cops coming up from Atlantic City on their way back to Boston. They were going to stop by and show me some photos," she said.

It was now Monday afternoon, sometime after 3 p.m., and the case was about to go into overdrive. The cops sitting on number 8 Highpoint Circle saw something they did not like— Philip Markoff, the tall, blond guy, and his fiancée had just exited the apartment building carrying a suitcase and a small backpack.

Boston Police caught a break when security cameras at two Boston hotels revealed a man the police later identified as Philip Markoff, calmly typing on his BlackBerry after leaving the scene.

Markoff revealed little emotion at his arraignment.

Philip Markoff with his attorney, John Salsberg.

Brandon Loboda

Phillip Markoff

No one suspected that a clean-cut student from sleepy Sherrill, New York, could become someone called "the Craigslist Killer."

Morgan Houston, a college friend of Markoff's, said she once had to fight off his aggressive advances.

Markoff receives the white coat of a doctor; his chosen profession made his arrest all the more shocking.

Julissa Brisman, who was fatally shot by the Craigslist Killer at the Westin Copley Hotel in Boston.

Julissa was a model and masseuse who did several lingerie shoots.

Trisha Leffler was the first to report the man who would become "the Craigslist Killer." Her information was vital in helping the police apprehend Philip Markoff.

left: Leffler was bound and robbed at the Westin Copley Place after making an appointment with a stranger over Craigslist. *right:* The Boston Marriott Copley, where Julissa Brisman met her killer on April 14, 2009.

Philip Markoff and Megan McAllister's engagement photo, taken from their wedding website. Megan never suspected her fiancé capable of any violence and soon after his arrest, she issued a statement stating, "He would not hurt a fly."

Markoff and McAllister met while volunteering at a hospital together, according to their wedding website. The site is no longer active.

Megan McAllister departing the Nashua Street Jail where Philip Markoff was held after his arrest.

Police staked out 8 Highpoint Circle in Quincy, Massachusetts, the upscale apartment building where Philip Markoff lived.

Suffolk County District Attorney Daniel F. Conley addresses the press after Markoff's arraignment.

John Salsberg, Philip Markoff's attorney, has won tough cases in the past.

Philip Markoff was hiding many secrets from his friends and family, including a profile on Alt.com, an "adult personals" website. Police sources confirmed this photograph was found on Markoff's computer.

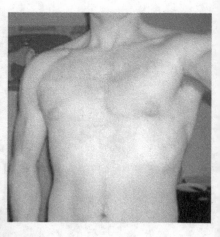

With its combination of murder, sex, and a clean-cut suspect, the "Craigslist Killer" story was irresistible to the media.

Few of Markoff's acquaintances could guess that the towheaded toddler and good student would one day be charged with murder and robbery.

13

Identification

With a trail of unmarked police cars around them, Phil Markoff and Megan McAllister began driving their Toyota Corolla south on I-95. The cops didn't know where they were going, but they knew it wasn't going to be long before they would be out of Massachusetts and into Rhode Island. That morning, Rhode Island authorities had released the newest batch of surveillance stills to the press, which was going nuts for the story. Those pictures were everywhere. Had they spooked the suspect into leaving town?

"There's a million things going through your head," Albert later told a reporter for the *Herald*. "Is he taking off because he saw the surveillance photos? It becomes intense."

Word was sent back to Police Commissioner Davis and District Attorney Conley. "We didn't know what he was up to at that time," Conley said. "The investigators on the scene reported to the police commissioner and me that the suspect was on the move, and we agreed we didn't want this guy leaving Massachusetts. He was traveling at a high rate of speed down Ninety-five. He was not going to be allowed to leave Massachusetts. We had enough evidence to do that. He was a person of interest at that point."

The two cops coming back from their weekend in Atlantic City were told to step on it—they were needed in Manhattan immediately, if not sooner. They were to pick up a clean photo of the suspect faxed to them—it was Phil Markoff's photo ID from Boston University. By this time, investigators had reached out to their brother officers in New York. A photo array was being prepared, and that was a whole story in itself.

DA Conley explained that, in his seven years on the job, he found that eyewitness identification was often wrong and he wanted to improve the process. His department consulted with Dr. Gary Wells, a psychology professor from Iowa State University. Wells told Conley that the best approach was to have the eight photos stacked on top of one another, like a deck of cards, and the witness would be asked to turn the cards over one at a time.

Furthermore, it was important that the person showing the witness the cards not have any knowledge of who the suspect was. Over the years, cops sometimes gave witnesses clues as to which photo to pick out, sometimes intentionally, sometimes not.

Conley wanted this photo array done strictly according to Dr. Wells's suggestions.

He did not want anything to possibly taint the identification process. For that reason, the photo array was going to be handled and supervised by an NYPD sergeant.

By the time the Boston and New York cops found one another and went to Trisha's room, it was approaching 4 p.m.

Markoff's car was getting closer and closer to the Massachusetts–Rhode Island border. The Boston PD had done a massive amount of work on the case, and they were not about to let him slip out of their jurisdiction. But the DA's office was insisting that Trisha make a positive identification. Everyone was on edge.

In New York, the two Boston cops stepped into the hallway as the NYPD sergeant stayed in Trisha's room and presented her with the photos, one on top of the other. Could she identify the man who had bound and robbed her? Trisha turned the cards once one at a time and did not hesitate. "I stopped on number five and said 'That's him,'" Trisha recalled. "As soon as I saw the picture, I started shaking. The cop from New York went out into the hallway and told them I made the identification."

One of the Boston cops already was on his cell phone to Lieutenant Detective Robert Merner, head of the homicide unit. Once he heard that Trisha had made a positive ID, Merner gave the order to the trailing cops to stop Markoff's car immediately.

In New York, the sergeant and the Boston cops were giving each other high fives. Trisha had only one question:

Do you have him in custody?

We do now.

Trisha said she made her identification at 4:03 p.m. Markoff's car was stopped on I-95 near Walpole, less than fifty miles from Rhode Island. It was 4:07 p.m.

14

Under Arrest

The moment Phil Markoff stepped out of his car on the shoulder of I-95, he and his bewildered fiancée were surrounded by a small army of police officers. They told them that the car was being seized, and they needed them to answer some questions. The couple would be escorted back to Boston Police headquarters in separate police cars.

Markoff was stoic and had no questions.

That in itself was suspicious. Megan had a more typical reaction to being stopped by several unmarked police cars—she was a bundle of nerves and wanted to know what the hell was going on. But the cops were asking, not answering, questions and they wanted to know where the couple was heading. Megan told them that they were going to Foxwoods casino in Connecticut for an overnight trip. When police searched Markoff's property, they found a blank check and forty-five $100 bills. It was a strong indication that Markoff was a regular at Foxwoods and had enjoyed more than the occasional hand of poker and blackjack.

Markoff said virtually nothing, and back at headquarters, he asked for a lawyer. It was clear he would need one—he was informed he was being arrested for the murder of Julissa Brisman and the armed robbery and kidnapping of Trisha Leffler.

Detectives Merner and Duff shifted their attention to Megan. They wanted to know more about Markoff and, specifically, her whereabouts for the previous week. She told them she'd been at her parents' home in Little Silver, New Jersey, getting treatment for a chronic back problem. Megan, who friends describe as sweet but sheltered, said she was barely aware of the Craigslist Killer case, although she did volunteer that her mother had warned her to be careful because "some guy had killed somebody up in Boston."

Merner and Duff didn't know what to make of Megan but felt sorry for her. They sensed that she was probably telling the truth about knowing nothing of her fiancé's activities, if indeed he was the killer. They broke the news to her gently. Her fiancé, Phil Markoff, was being arrested as the Craigslist Killer. He would be arraigned on murder charges the following day. Megan began crying and told the police that she wanted to go home to her parents in New Jersey. She asked if she might borrow a computer to buy plane tickets online. They sat her in front of a computer and then later drove her to Logan Airport, where she caught a flight to New Jersey.

"She just wanted to go home," Duff said.

There was no indication that Megan knew anything about the crimes Markoff was accused of, and police allowed her to leave. They, however, had a long night ahead of them. They secured a search warrant and began picking their way through the $1,400-a-month rental the couple shared. It was a long but fruitful night, full of the kinds of discoveries that can make a cop's day.

15

Is the Doctor a Killer?

On Monday evening, Boston police commissioner Ed Davis and Suffolk County district attorney Dan Conley held a press conference to announce that they had arrested a suspect in the Craigslist Killer case. The nightmare of a modern-day Jack the Ripper roaming the tourist-filled streets of downtown Boston seemingly had ended as quickly as it had begun. The three crimes connected to Craigslist and the tall blond stranger had occurred in only seven days, and now, days after the last incident, the Boston PD was broadcasting its prize catch to a very hungry media. The news was *so* good that Commissioner Davis could not help kvelling: "We are very, very happy to have this man off the street in such a timely way."

Reporters asked if the alleged killer had been tracked electronically. "We followed a multitude of avenues, high-tech leads and old-fashioned shoe leather," Conley said. "We obtained identifications and matched IP addresses to physical locations. The investigation is not over and we will not rest until Julissa Brisman's killer is held responsible for his crimes."

The press conference ended, but the cops braced themselves—they knew what was coming. Based on what they had now learned about Phil Markoff, the cops were aware that news of his arrest would send this already hot story into the stratosphere. Phil Markoff was the most unlikely of murder suspects, and not only because he was blond and preppy. The real shocker was that Markoff was studying to be a doctor at the prestigious Boston University School of Medicine. The irony was so heavy-handed as to be suspect, but there it was: Markoff was training to save lives as a doctor in the emergency room at Boston Medical Center, the same ER where Julissa Brisman died of three gunshot wounds, allegedly at Markoff's own hand.

The press went crazy.

Veteran crime reporter Maria Cramer remembers a sense of wonder at hearing about Markoff. "This is a very unusual suspect here," she said. "A man nobody would ever suspect of doing something like this. A man who by all means *shouldn't* do something like this. This is somebody who wanted to be a healer. This is somebody who wanted to help people. That's why people become doctors. And so when you find out that somebody who's heading toward such a respectable field is instead hurting people, it shocks anybody. He is by all accounts what we would consider a good citizen. He has no criminal record. He was an ambitious, intelligent man who had a future ahead of him. Comes from a good, supportive, loving family in upstate New York. And if police are correct that this is the man who did this, then he has been leading a double life."

And that double life was only beginning to come into focus. While reporters and producers worked the phones and surfed the Internet to obtain every scrap of information that existed on Markoff, television trucks and print reporters raced to Quincy and set up shop at number 8 Highpoint Circle. In another delicious twist, this couple was the sort of upscale tenant that managers of Highpoint Circle had been trying to attract—but they hadn't counted on one of them turning up as a murder suspect.

Jonathan Uva, who lived next door to Markoff and Megan, admitted that he was shocked by the arrest but he said that Markoff, who was friendly enough, rarely talked about himself. "I can't even put into words what I'm feeling right now," he said. "Knowing him and hearing all of this . . . it just doesn't connect to the guy I know. I don't really know what to think.

"We all met at the clubhouse for a holiday function. Every month or so they have functions for something or other, and him and his girlfriend were there. He looked like a clean-cut guy. I had read the articles [about the Craigslist Killer], but you couldn't see exactly what he looked like."

Mike Dye, another neighbor, said he was so overwhelmed by what reporters were telling him that he couldn't gauge his own reaction. Dye, an athletic-looking twentysomething, had felt that Markoff was, well, just like him. Dye had even invited Markoff to his Super Bowl party, and had tried to get the aspiring doctor to hang out with him. "He seemed like a nice guy," Dye said. "Normal, down to earth. I like to think I'm a pretty good judge of character, and I like to hang out with people who are similar to myself."

He said his interactions with Markoff were so mundane that he couldn't recall them with any specificity. "I didn't realize he was a student. He was friendly. As far as I knew, he lived here with his girlfriend. I only saw her once, though. I always saw him in the elevators. I haven't seen him though in the last three weeks, which is weird.

"I still don't know how to take it. I don't know what my reaction is going to be tomorrow. We leave our doors unlocked around here. It's a pretty tight-knit group."

Perhaps tellingly, no one at the complex—at least no one who spoke to reporters—seemed particularly close to Markoff, and when all their comments were added together, he sounded for all the world like a frat boy without an ounce of personality. His family, of course, claimed he was a good boy, everything you'd want in a son.

Markoff's grandfather Jerome Markoff, a lawyer from Maryland, could not believe the news. "I'm shocked," he told the *Boston Globe*. "This is not my grandson. I know my grandson. I hate to see a rush to judgment. I hate to see it. He's a wonderful boy, absolutely wonderful, and couldn't be better. I'm proud of him and proud of his abilities as a medical student. He always wanted to be a doctor.

"He's never gotten into trouble, never, never, never. That's why it's shocking."

"What we've heard about Philip Markoff is that he was almost unremarkable," said Cramer. "I mean, nobody doubted his intelligence. But it was sort of this pat kind of thing you normally hear about somebody who's accused of something like this. 'Nice guy.' 'Never saw it coming.' 'I'm shocked.'

"We know so little right now, even though in some ways, we know so much."

As they had with Julissa, reporters and producers attacked Markoff's Facebook page with gusto and began contacting the hundreds of people Markoff listed as friends. The outlines of Markoff's public life began to take shape. Nearly everyone remarked on Markoff's superior intelligence. He had graduated from the UAlbany in three years, polishing off a Bachelor of Science degree in biology in 2007, and graduated summa cum laude. the *Boston Globe* even had a photograph of Markoff in its archives taken on White Coat Day, the first day that would-be doctors at the BU Medical School try on the white coat that is the emblem of their new profession. The camera captured Markoff as he was slipping on the coat, his eyes nearly closed in jubilation. It is a photo of a man on top—he has an ear-to-ear grin that would make the Cheshire cat envious, and looks like one of the happiest people alive. And why not? It is difficult to gain entry to medical school anywhere, and here Markoff was at one of the finest schools in the country. Success was there for the taking.

In a certain sense, Phil Markoff was following in the footsteps of his father, Dr. Richard Markoff, a dentist who practices in Syracuse, New York. Markoff's father and mother, Susan Haynes, divorced when Markoff was very young. Hometown friends said they'd never met Dr. Markoff, but described Ms. Haynes as a "sweetheart." Phil was raised by his mother, who after the divorce resettled in Sherrill, New York, a place proud to be the smallest city in New York State with a population of only 3,150. It is only about thirty-five miles east of Syracuse and considered a bedroom community of that college town.

Susan soon remarried a banker named Gary Carroll, who is close to Phil. Susan and Gary had a baby girl in 1991, when Phil was only five years old. While Phil lived with his mother, his older brother, Jon, lived with the boys' father. Phil's mother was a stay-at-home mom when her children were young, but eventually got a job in the gift shop of the nearby Turning Stone Resort Casino. Susan and Gary Carroll eventually divorced, but both still live in Sherrill.

Markoff's small-town roots, his father the dentist, and his much-admired brainpower were interesting, but didn't touch on the *real* question. Everyone wanted to know, if Markoff *was* the Craigslist Killer, what was going on in his mind? His life—now a complex puzzle—

needed to be deconstructed because, at first blush, it made no sense. "This is a suspect who, by any stretch of the imagination, has everything going for him," said Maria Cramer. "He has everything that you could possibly want out of life. And according to the police, he blew it. That's something that I can't understand. I don't know what kind of demons you have if you would give up something like that. If this is indeed the person, it's shocking that he would go to this level. Getting into the head of somebody like this is something that I'd love to do. But I don't know if you could ever understand the motives behind a crime like this where you basically are a predator." But the press was going to try.

In the meantime, with Markoff out of reach, the story veered toward his beautiful, blonde fiancée, Megan McAllister. What must she be thinking? Reporters turned to the Internet, which, once again, did not disappoint. Megan's Facebook page was bombarded with messages from the media. A couple of quick

Google searches later, journalists learned that
Markoff and Megan were planning to be married on August 14, 2009, and as many couples
do, had set up an extensive and somewhat pre-
cious wedding website for friends and family.

That website was shut down by midmorning the next day, but it had already become required reading for every reporter who was hot
on Markoff's trail—and it provided plenty of
information about the couple that otherwise
would not have been readily available. Reporters made sure to capture screen grabs from the
website before it disappeared, gobbled up every
detail they could, and sent out bulletins to
eager readers and viewers who could not get
enough of this white-hot story.

16

Wedding Bells

The home page of the Markoff-McAllister wedding website featured the now iconic photograph of the glowing couple looking like a million bucks. There stands handsome Phil, beaming while he holds his future wife, Megan, his hands on her hips. She is stunning in a black dress, blonde hair draped nearly to her breasts, her head and body tilted back toward Phil, her strapping fiancé. They look perfect set against the website's mauve background. And there at the top of the page was a looming countdown clock noting how many days, hours, minutes, and yes, even seconds until the two became husband and wife. One can only imagine what Phil, allegedly reading the erotic services listings on Craigslist, thought about his bachelorhood being counted down by the second.

The web pages celebrated the couple's courtship. The two of them "met cute" toting bodily fluids around Albany Medical Center. *We . . . spent about 2 weeks pushing stretchers down hallways and bringing blood and urine samples to pathology together before our first date on November 11, 2005.* At that point, Megan was a senior at UAlbany and Phil was a sophomore. They even lived in side-by-side apartment buildings, but had never met until September 19, 2005, when they began volunteering at the hospital.

It was love at first sight. After that, the two spent more and more time together. They both belonged to the same coed college fraternity, Phi Delta Epsilon, and on May 17, 2008, Phil proposed to Megan on a horse-and-buggy ride. After they became engaged, they moved to Quincy, although Megan often spent weeks back home in New Jersey preparing for their sumptuous wedding. She also hoped to be a doctor and was planning to attend an offshore medical school on the Caribbean island of St. Kitts in the fall of 2009. Their lives were busy, and the website noted that their real honeymoon would not take place for another eight years, when the two planned to go to Tahiti. In the meantime, they put it to their prospective guests: *Which all-inclusive exotic honeymoon location should we choose?* The choices were: Murrells Inlet, South Carolina; Saratoga Springs, New York; Boothbay Harbor, Maine; or the Mohegan Sun hotel and casino in Connecticut.

There were eleven quiz pages in all, measuring one's knowledge of the couple, including where Phil proposed and who had designed Megan's wedding dress. Was it Vera Wang or Priscilla of Boston? Was Megan's favorite drink the Cosmo or cherry limeade? Reading all this, you had to feel sorry for Megan, a seemingly naive young woman blindsided by a man who reportedly was not at all what he appeared. Other than being left at the altar, this was a bride's worst nightmare, and must have been bitterly disappointing. Judging from the website's hype, it's clear that Megan was anticipating the type of fairy-tale wedding many women dream of when they are little girls. There were nineteen people in the wedding party, and the ceremony was set to take place at sunset on a beach in Long Branch, New Jersey. A reception would follow at McLoone's Pier House, and guests would dance to a Bruce Springsteen tribute band called the B-Street Band. Megan was, after all, a Jersey girl.

We look forward to spending our special day with you.

By emailing and phoning anyone and everyone who was invited to the wedding, reporters learned that Megan's three older brothers had met Phil and, by all accounts, had considered him a wonderful guy, fully worthy of their little sister. But Phil had yet to even meet Megan's bridesmaids, her closest friends from high school, and with only four months to go before the ceremony, *that* struck some as odd.

The website was quickly taken down after news of Markoff's arrest broke, but not before someone with the username creampie surprise posed this question on the site's guest registry: *I have a question about the hotel you guys are holding the wedding in . . . has the groom killed anyone there yet?*

Megan clearly was angry, and vowed to stand by her man, at least according to two emails she sent in those early morning hours of Tuesday, April 21. To the *Boston Herald*, she wrote: *Philip is a beautiful man inside and out. He is intelligent, loyal, and the best friend a woman could ask for. He would not hurt a fly. Unfortunately the Boston police try to make money out of these things and release things without my knowledge or consent. I will stand by Philip as I know he is innocent. I love him now and always will.*

There was also an email sent to ABC News's *Good Morning America*: *Unfortunately, you were given wrong information as was the public. All I have to say to you is Philip is a beautiful person inside and out and could not hurt a fly! A police officer in Boston (or many) is trying to make big bucks by selling this false story to the TV stations. What else is new? Philip is an intelligent man who is just trying to live his life so if you could leave us alone we would greatly appreciate it. We expect to marry in August and share a wonderful, meaningful life together.*

One of the detectives later said he was upset that Megan blasted the cops, saying, "We were very nice to her."

By morning, when the authorities told everyone what the police had found in their search of Markoff's apartment, Megan's emails would sound hollow indeed. And if Megan was experiencing the sleeplessness of someone whose life turned upside down, the same could not be said for Markoff. According to sources, Markoff seemed to have not a care in the world that first night in jail: He slept like a baby.

17

Inside Markoff's Apartment

Trisha Leffler was one of the first to know about the incriminating evidence allegedly found in Phil Markoff's Highpoint Circle apartment. That's because detectives checked in with her while they were conducting their search. Trisha was one of the cops' best witnesses, and they wanted to run a few things by her. "One of the detectives called me from the apartment and asked what kind of camera and credit cards he had taken," Trisha said. "He asked for a description of the panties again."

She had previously described in detail the two pairs of underwear she said Markoff had taken from her hotel room: both were thongs—one pair was white and cream, and the second was pink with black bows. "The cops said they found both pairs," she said, "and I told them I did not want them back."

When the media first reported that the police had found two pairs of panties, they assumed the underwear belonged to two different women, but Trisha asserts that she was told both pairs were exactly what she described and both belonged to her.

Understandably, she is proud of assisting the cops. "If I wouldn't have come forward on that night, I don't think this case would be where it is today," she said. "If I were a coward, they wouldn't have caught him so quickly. I didn't want him to do this to anyone else."

Trisha says her camera was not found but her two American Express gift cards, as well as the knife and gun she had described were located in Markoff's apartment, according to what the cops told her. Cops told Trisha that Markoff had been using her gift cards in and around Boston. They did not tell Trisha *where* they found the gun—but that soon became front-page news. Markoff allegedly hid the gun inside a hollowed-out copy of the classic medical school textbook *Gray's Anatomy*. For the press, it was almost too good to be true.

That Tuesday afternoon, April 21, Markoff was set to be arraigned on murder, robbery, and kidnapping charges at 4 p.m. inside the Boston Municipal Court. But before the hearing was convened, information about the evidence that police allegedly had found in Markoff's apartment began to leak out. One journalist, wondering aloud how difficult it would be to hollow out a textbook of that size, was answered by another: "He probably used his scalpel." Somehow, that made sense. Maria Cramer and other reporters learned that plastic zip tie handcuffs, the same type used to bind

Trisha and Julissa, were allegedly found inside the Highpoint Circle apartment, as was duct tape.

Finding the potential murder weapon hidden inside *the* medical textbook used by every aspiring doctor once again highlighted the very essence of why so many found the Markoff story so captivating. If the allegations against him were true, then Phil Markoff personified the dramatic and age-old confrontation between good and evil, as though angels and demons were fighting for control of Markoff's soul. On one hand, he was an aspiring healer; on the other, a potential killer.

And the allegation that Trisha's underwear was found in Markoff's apartment made everyone wonder anew what was going through Markoff's mind during his crimes. Was he really just out to rob these women, or was something much darker at play?

Dr. Casey Jordan, a criminologist and attorney from Connecticut, was one of the first to speculate that Markoff's motives were far more complex than first suspected. "From the beginning, they have always listed 'robbery' as a motive, but there is a sexual component to these crimes, because all of the victims were advertising sexual or erotic services on Craigslist," she said. "The idea that you would go to all this trouble . . . just to rob a person never made sense. The sexual component is there. The fact that they found souvenirs of a sexual nature shows that there is an underpinning of thrill that really transcends the idea that it was just a money-motivated robbery.

"I believe he wanted the money, but the underlying theme is the thrill. The idea of arranging it, getting something for nothing, getting someone to meet you there, getting someone to trust you, to tie up the victims— perhaps there was sexual contact, perhaps not— but you have that idea that this is about control . . . and sexual thrill all wrapped up in this guy's psyche. . . . This guy has a character, personality issue. He needs the rush of a confrontation, of feeling he is getting something over on someone, getting something for nothing. The idea that he would meet these girls and go to great lengths to do it when he could just rob someone at a cash machine shows that this crime is multifaceted. The idea that he is the stereotype of a person who would not do this also really gives him the rush. The idea that no one would suspect him—I'm sure he feels he was going to get away with it—that's why he got so careless. The idea of [taking] undergarments from the victims again shows that he wanted to remember the event. Something about the event, whether it was sexual or thrilling, is something he wanted to relive by touching the souvenir. There's way more about this crime than a money-motivated robbery."

Dr. Jordan's words ring very true when one remembers that, according to Trisha, Markoff paused after tying her to the bathroom door in her hotel, to unzip her suitcase and remove a second pair of underwear. He already had one pair of her panties in his pocket, the pair that had been lying on a pile of dirty clothing, but he went out of his way and spent more time in the room than he needed to, just to rifle through her intimates so he could find and take a second pair. It was risky, but if Markoff was after a thrill, he got exactly what he wanted. Also, let's not forget the secondary thrill—he had Trisha totally under his control, bound and soon to be gagged. Phil Markoff has a much more deviant sexual side than anyone knew, and as the weeks went by and more information was developed and uncovered, it would turn out that Dr. Jordan's depiction of Markoff as an out-of-control thrill seeker looked to be very much on target.

But on the afternoon of Tuesday, April 21, all anyone really cared about was getting a look at Phil Markoff in the flesh as he was led into court for his arraignment.

18

First Look

There were maybe a hundred people packed into the fifth-floor courtroom of Judge Paul K. Leary when Phil Markoff was led in, but none of them was a relative. His fiancée, Megan, was hundreds of miles away at her parents' home in Little Silver, New Jersey, and there was no sign of any friends, either. Markoff stood alone as he faced murder, robbery, and kidnapping charges; the only people there to support him were his de-

fense team, lead counsel John Salsberg and co-
counsel Margaret Fox. Salsberg, a well- regarded
attorney, had been appointed by the court earlier in the day after Markoff told court person-
nel that he was indigent, with no money to call
upon for a defense. He said that he'd been living off $130,000 in student loans obtained for
his medical school education.

Standing in for Julissa Brisman was her father, Hector Brisman, who sat in the front row.
The rest of her family and her friends were
down in New York for her wake, which was
scheduled for the following day.

All eyes were locked on Markoff, who was
wearing a pair of tan trousers and a blue-and-
white-striped shirt. His clothing looked a bit
rumpled after his night in the Nashua Street
Jail, but except for the handcuffs and leg irons,
he looked like an office worker on "casual Friday." He towered over the court officers near
him, which gave everyone an idea of his size.
More than one cop said quietly that a guy this
size had not needed to shoot and kill Julissa

Brisman—not when he outweighed her by at least a hundred pounds.

Maria Cramer observed him closely, but his face revealed no outward emotion. "He was shackled at the ankles and at the wrists," she said. "He looked calm. His shoulders were slumped. There was no strong reaction. You know, his face was expressionless is how I'd describe it. And he sat down next to his lawyer. While his face didn't really change, his body language indicated that he was nervous. He was breathing rapidly, he was blinking a lot. He didn't look calm when you studied him closely."

Assistant District Attorney Jennifer Hickman laid out the state's case against Markoff. "Your Honor, based on the forensic evidence from the crime scenes both at the Westin Hotel as well as the Copley Marriot Hotel, we received information, forensic evidence, not only from the crime scene but also from electronic and cellular communications, Internet communications, as well as surveillance video from two hotels, Your Honor," she said. "We know that it is the defendant before you, Philip Markoff, who on April 10, 2009, brought and tied up a woman while she was at the Westin Hotel and that this is the defendant who, on April 14, 2009, bashed in the head of Julissa Brisman and shot her three times at close range.

"There's a commonality, Your Honor, between both of these two particular cases, that being that both of these women advertised services for 'masseuse' on Craigslist, both of them were working out of hotels in downtown Boston, both women were bound or were attempted to be bound, both of the females were unarmed, and in the use of this particular incident, not only were these individuals bound but a gun was used as well.

"From the physical evidence that was obtained or recovered during the course of that particular hotel room [it] appears that Ms. Brisman put up a fight. She sustained blunt head trauma to her skull. She also received three gunshots at close range. Two of those gunshots were through and through. The third one was lodged in her left hip. One of the injuries, the bullet that went through Ms. Brisman's heart, according to the medical examiner, would've caused her death immediately. We know from video surveillance that the individual who killed Ms. Brisman walked calmly out of that Marriot Copley Hotel.

"During the course of the investigation, we've been able to track Internet information relative to an account used to make one of the appointments in this investigation. We were able to track the computer used to make up an email account to an IP address to Philip Markoff at an address in Quincy. We also know during the course of the investigation, Your Honor, that there was contact between this individual as well as with at least one of the victims. Your Honor, based on what the investigation was, a search warrant was executed last night at the defendant's home. Recovered during the execution of the search warrant was a semiautomatic firearm as well as ammunition, as well as items that were used or consistent with what were used to [bind] the victim in the Westin Hotel incident and were attempted to be used on Ms. Brisman during the incident at the Marriot Copley.

"Based on the violent nature of this case, Your Honor, as well as the brutal murder of an unarmed female, who appeared to have been fighting for her life as she was pulling off and trying to get away from this defendant, I ask that the defendant be held without bail on the murder complaint, Your Honor, and [with] a million-dollar cash bail on the kidnapping and armed robbery complaint."

Markoff's lawyer, John Salsberg, who has a track record for successfully defending seemingly hopeless cases, later told reporters, "Philip Markoff is not guilty of the charges. He has family support. Philip is bearing up. It's obviously a difficult time for anybody under these circumstances, for the charges that have been brought against him . . . he pleaded 'not guilty.' He is not guilty."

Judge Leary agreed with the prosecutor

that there would be no bail on the murder charge but set bail on the robbery and kidnapping charges at $250,000. It hardly mattered— Markoff would be calling the Nashua Street Jail home for the immediate future. Within hours, Markoff also had been suspended from Boston University, but that was the least of his problems.

The Suffolk County district attorney held a press conference after the hearing to let everyone know what he thought of Phil Markoff: "We're dealing with somebody who is fairly clever, who certainly made efforts to hide himself from authorities by creating email addresses to contact these young women, and also choosing women who were vulnerable, women who were perhaps living on life's margins, who perhaps would not contact authorities if they were victimized, and this is the type of individual we're dealing with, someone who is willing to abuse women, to dominate them, to hurt them to get what he wants."

Conley was repeating a working theory of

the case—that Markoff had chosen women who were either prostitutes or working just at the edge of the law because he felt they would not report the robberies to the authorities. Of course, that proved to be a false assumption, given that both Trisha Leffler and Amber, the lap dancer in Rhode Island, both reported the crimes immediately after they occurred. Cramer said the impression she took away from the hearing and the press conference was that the man police described as the Craigslist Killer "has moved in the way a predator moves. And it's very stealthy," she said. "He really chose his victims carefully. He wasn't just going after anybody. So that requires a high level of sophistication, looking for these people. In the robberies themselves, it sounds like he went after people that he could dominate very, very, very easily.

"You are stalking people. You're not just going into a liquor store [or] robbing a bank at gunpoint. You're really going out of your way to frighten people."

Conley publicly asked any victims of Markoff's to come forward and he promised they would not be prosecuted for prostitution or any sort of illegal sexual activity. "There is a possibility that there are others out there," he said. "So in my public comments over the last couple of days, I've asked anyone who's been contacted by Philip Markoff, perhaps was even approached in a hotel and robbed by Philip Markoff, to please let us know. I'm sure that these young women, if there are any others, would be worried about any possible prosecution on our end. We're not concerned about prosecuting these young women for offering masseuse services, or perhaps even other services, what I'm more concerned about, while I don't approve of that conduct, what I'm more concerned about is prosecuting Philip Markoff for any other incidents that he may have committed. Now, he may not have committed any others, but if there are any others, we'd like to know about it. So we're urging anyone that has possibly been victimized in a similar way to come forward. Let us take a look at that evidence and then move from there.

To help make Conley's point, authorities the next day took the extraordinary step of posting their own ad in the erotic services section of Boston's Craigslist:

Were you attacked or robbed at a Boston-area hotel after placing an ad on Craigslist? If so, you may have information that could aid the investigation into the April 10 armed robbery of a woman at the Westin Copley Place Hotel and the April 14 murder of a woman at the Marriott Copley Place Hotel. Both victims were attacked by a prospective client who had contacted them through ads placed on Craigslist.

Someone did come forward, but it was not what the authorities were expecting—and they were as shocked as anyone.

19

Was It the Gambling?

Once the initial legal proceedings were over, and the initial shock of the arrest had worn off, the question everyone wanted to know was: Why? You could scarcely ask the gods for more than they had given Markoff.

"I would describe him as being the perfect all-American kid, you know what I mean?" said Joe Moura, a Boston-based private investigator. "Lovely girlfriend. Ready to get married.

Going to med school. I mean, he's got a terrific future ahead of him. And I'm sure that typically every parent would look at him, and say, 'You know, if I'm gonna have a son, I'd want one just like him.' "

If you were to take a measure of the man before the arrest, you would have to have said, based on every societal indicator, that Phil Markoff had life licked.

Why, if the charges were true, would someone blow all of that on this series of bone-headed robberies? How could someone so smart be so dumb? "I've had a lot of clients that are by all accounts terrific guys, and for some reason fall on hard times. Something snaps in their head. And they do something terribly stupid," Moura said. "What led to that? Usually, you go into drug problems. They get into drugs."

Before the arrest, police investigators had thought the same thing. Looking at the crime spree, they believed the person responsible was so desperate that there was a real possibility he was driven by a need for drugs. But there were zero signs that Markoff was a drug addict, and when he told the court that he was broke, authorities began to speculate that his true addiction might be gambling. It wasn't so far-fetched. Markoff and Megan were on their way to Foxwoods casino when he was stopped and arrested, and friends from high school and college mentioned that he frequently played poker, although never for very much money.

And then there was Jamie, the young mother from Cape Cod who had been sitting at the blackjack table in Foxwoods casino the same night that the Craigslist Killer tried to rob Amber, the lap dancer in Warwick. Jamie said she was watching her toddler after the Markoff arrest and happened to see him on television. "I thought, 'Where do I know that guy from?'" she said. "And then I realized it was him. I said, 'Oh my God, that was the weird guy sitting next to us at Foxwoods.' I was creeped out. He was a very, very, *very* strange man."

Soon enough, police sources were telling

reporters that they were looking into the possibility that Markoff had gambling debts, which may have fueled his alleged crime spree. ABC News, in particular, ran stories on its website that claimed Markoff made at least three trips to the casino in April, including one on April 16, two days after Julissa's murder and the same day he allegedly tried to hold up the lap dancer in Warwick. That matches Jamie's story. But what does not make sense about the report is that it claims Markoff won $5,300 on April 16. When Jamie watched him, he was losing—possibly a motive for planning and trying to carry out another robbery that very evening.

Moura speculated that it was not gambling *debts* that had gotten Markoff into trouble. It was his gambling *habit*. "He had a terrible gambling habit," the private eye said. "There's no evidence that I'm aware of at this time that he actually had debts that he had to pay off. No bookies or loan sharks, that type of thing. There's no evidence of that. And I suspect what was happening here is that he needed to feed that habit, and getting the cash to be able to go immediately to the casino and gamble it."

But Maria Cramer remains skeptical that gambling was Markoff's real motive. "I haven't been told by any of his friends or people who knew him that he had gambling debts or that he was a heavy gambler, but he definitely enjoyed going to casinos, playing poker," she said. "That we have heard from friends . . . there have been reports of gambling debts, but police haven't confirmed that. He's not talking. Police . . . spoke with him for less than thirty minutes before he asked for a lawyer."

There was also no apparent trigger for why, if he is indeed guilty, Markoff acted *when* he did, and that's what psychologists look for. Why did Markoff allegedly begin his spree on April 10? Why not six months earlier or six months later? What was the motivating factor? No one knew, but as people begin to dig deep into Markoff's activities, it was clear he had more to hide than a suspected gambling addiction.

Even in those first days after his arrest, reporters running a Google search of Markoff's phone number came across a Craigslist ad, apparently posted by him. Police confirmed they had found it too but, like everyone else, didn't know what to make of it. Under the heading *Ebony Erotic Massage*, the ad said *Taking my last appointment* and encouraged customers to call Markoff's number. Clearly, there was a lot going on behind the expressionless face Markoff showed in court. For the moment, until authorities learned more about Markoff's secret life, this was just another in a series of tantalizing clues.

20

Happy Birthday . . .
RIP

The day after Philip Markoff appeared in court, the family of Julissa Brisman held a wake for her at the R. G. Ortiz Funeral Home in New York at Broadway and West 189th Street. The family kept the media and camera crews across the street, feeling too overcome to speak. A long line of friends, family, and the curious who had heard of Julissa's untimely death lined up to pay their respects. Inside, the air was filled with the wailing of Julissa's mother, Carmen. "Why not me? Why her?" she cried. Her words were in Spanish, her grief universal. "She was only twenty-five. She was just beginning to live her life."

Overwhelmed by her oldest daughter's death, Carmen asked the Suffolk County District Attorney's Office to release a statement in her name:

> I feel very much relieved that the man who did this is in custody and will not be able to do this horrible thing to another family. Our family has been devastated by the loss of our beautiful daughter Julissa. We are a close family, and Julissa called us every day. We won't be getting those calls anymore. Over the past few days, people have told us the many ways in which Julissa helped them. Her friends say Julissa was like a bright light, full of energy and optimism, always ready to help other people. These words mean so much to us.
>
> The feeling of losing my daughter in this

way, and the pain she must have felt, will haunt me for the rest of my life. She won't live to see her dreams. We will hold Julissa in our hearts every day.

Julissa's friends defended her memory against widespread rumors that she was a prostitute. "She was not a hooker," said Edna Cales, who lived in the same building. "She was a good girl. It's a bunch of lies they're saying about her."

Mark Pines, Julissa's ubiquitous friend, was there at her funeral, comforting her mother and saying that he hoped the knowledge of what happened to Julissa would prevent other girls tempted by easy money from following the same path. He said Julissa had been careful with her clients, but sadly, it had made no difference.

Many of those who attended the funeral had had no idea of Julissa's personal life, now spread across the front pages of every newspaper in the country. Her cousins Jenny and Daisy Guzman said they didn't know that

Julissa was a masseuse and didn't think her mother had any idea, either.

Among those who came forward to speak on her behalf was James Destri, one of the founding members of the 1970s rock group Blondie, who met Julissa when they were both taking classes at City College. "She was dedicated," Destri told the *Daily News*. "This is a girl who was trying to turn her life around. She had her demons, and she dealt with them. We all had backgrounds, but she was a really nice kid. She was sweet. I want people to know she was more than 'the masseuse.' "

In light of the fact that Julissa lived much of her life online and met her death through an online classified ad, it seemed only fitting that the most poignant outpourings of grief were posted on her Facebook wall. In the days immediately after her murder, her Facebook friends were in shock and could only post sad-face emoticons and *RIP*. But after the initial shock wore off, the personal messages heralding Julissa's spirit began in earnest:

Julie: Juju, I'm in shock!! Why didn't u come to me? . . . now you'll be with the angels. How could this have happened?

Sabrina: that sucker will get his justice.

Beth: I loved you when you were a crazy brazen blonde, I loved you as a stunning studios brunette in AA. I'm so sorry this happened to you.

Jazmine: I don't even know what to say. Seems like just yesterday we were talking and hanging out. I will miss you sooooo much . . . just know that wherever you are you are lighting up the room right now with your beautiful self and energy.

Annie: I remember meeting you when I had just three days and was shaking like a leaf . . . terrified of everything. You came up to me and we clicked right away. You were soo sweet. Rest in peace beautiful . . . you are missed and loved and in everyone's prayers.

Sabrina: I will so miss your positivity and adorable comments, and every time I think of you just makes me so damn mad at that bastard . . .

Max: R.I.P. babe. I can't fucking believe this shit happened to you. You were a great friend and an amazing person. I wish u listened to me at least one of those times when I told you about all those perverted fkin assholes. I should've tried harder. I will miss you with all my heart. . . . I'll do my best to make sure that motherfucker who shot you gets his balls cut off and stuffed down his throat. . . .

Jennifer: Tricky this thing we call life. You always dream of being famous. Now more are aware of who you

are. Too bad it had to be this
way.

And then, on April 25, the day Julissa would
have turned twenty-six years old, she was instead placed in the ground, her final resting
place.

Her friend KiKi wrote this on Facebook:

Happy Birthday my hunny bunz! I wish you
were here so we can celebrate your birthday
as planned, but I will still celebrate it with a
VIRGIN strawberry daiquiri, just for you
☺ I miss you sooo much! Makes me sad to
think that you're getting buried on your
birthday ☹ RIP my angel.
Xoxoxoxoxoxoxoxoxo

21

Pleasantville

Hundreds of miles away from Manhattan, Phil Markoff's family and hometown friends in upstate New York could hardly believe what they were hearing about someone who had lived among them for years.

The residents of the city of Sherrill are in shock and disbelief as one of their own has been charged with a horrific crime five hours away from this tightly knit community.

That was the lead paragraph in the story carried by *The Oneida Daily Dispatch* on the day after local boy Phil Markoff was arrested, and there was not an ounce of hyperbole in the story—residents were overwhelmed by news that seemed inconceivable.

"I think it was Monday morning, I got a phone call from my father at like eight," said Dave Lipke, who went to school with Markoff from second grade through high school.

Lipke did not take the call from his father, but he couldn't ignore the chatter from the next room, where two of his roommates were carrying on about something. "I heard them awake and chirpin' away and just talkin' about something excitedly," Lipke said. "I was like, 'What's going on?' And they're like 'Philip Markoff is on TV.' They were just freakin' out about it. Like, we were shocked. No one could believe it."

Lipke's family had moved from Reno when

he was in second grade, and virtually the first person he met in Sherrill was Phil Markoff— the teacher had seated them in alphabetical order. He had been around Markoff for eleven years of his life, and would have had no inkling that Phil was capable of anything like this. Phil, whom Lipke described as a "great" bowler and member of the school team, showed a temper once in a while when he didn't get a strike or a spare, but that was about it. "Each new day it seems like something else comes up with Phil and it's just mind-boggling," he said. "Like, never in a million years would I have pictured him doing anything violent, let alone tying people up, robbing 'em and killing 'em, as it appears. I mean this is just unreal."

Almost everyone in Sherrill felt the same way because the town is not only the smallest town in New York State but also, apparently, one of the most placid. To get an idea of what Sherrill is like, all you really need to know is that locals sometimes refer to it as Pleasantville, after the 1998 Toby Maguire film of the same

name about two present-day teenagers who get
sucked into their television set to a small 1950s
town where everyone is pleasant and everything is black and white—literally. That's Sherrill.

It is a reference that Robert Comis, the city
manager of Sherrill, heartily endorses. "We just
have a kind of hometown feel when you're
here," he said. "The close knitness [sic] of the
community. It's that kind of feel."

Comis said the town has such a "comfortable" feel that no one locks their doors, never
mind worrying about a big-city problem like
the Craigslist Killer. It's a good bet that before
Markoff's name was associated with the crimes,
Comis and many others in the town probably
never even heard about Boston's problems.
Asked what it's like living in Sherrill, the city
manager ticked off Tuesday-night concerts, the
friendly people, a Memorial Day parade, and "a
wonderful fireworks display at the end of July."

Sherrill, he added, is also known in some
quarters as the "Silver City," because for a while,

the famous Oneida flatware was manufactured in its environs, but those days are over. The Oneida Community was a religious community that became infamous for its belief in non-monogamous sex and planned children. To this day, the town is home to the Oneida Community Mansion House, a gorgeous brick building that is a combination of large public rooms and thirty-five private apartments. Markoff's mother, Susan Haynes, lives in one of those apartments, having moved on from the house where Phil and his younger sister were raised.

City Manager Comis said, the city "has a rich history of supporting its kids. . . . Even within our city budgets, we make sure that they have parks to play in and proper equipment. A couple of years ago, we bought a community center and we've been renovating that. So, yeah. We're very much supportive of the children."

Markoff was one of those children. He went to local schools and graduated from Vernon-Verona-Sherrill High School in 2004 with 150

other students where he was a member of the
National Honor Society, Youth Court, and the
golf and bowling teams. He also apparently ex-
celled in poker, which he mentioned in his
yearbook, bequeathing his "playing skills" to a
friend.

Andrew Hookway was a member of that
class. He says he went to elementary school as
well as high school with Phil, saw him virtually
every day, and talked to him frequently, although he did not know all that much about
him. "He was just a great person to be around.
I wanna say he was, you know, just this guy, an
average high schooler," Hookway said. "I
wouldn't say that he's creepy at all. He just
seemed normal. There was nothing at all that
made Phil Markoff out of the ordinary. . . .
Sometimes there's people who stick out as
being very introverted and very nerdy. And he
was neither of those extremes. He was completely average."

It's become something of a cliché to describe
murderers that way, and yet Hookway could not

find the words to speak of his friend in any other way. He repeated what those in town said, that Phil was a good kid who went through an early growth spurt and seemed a little physically awkward but who was a good enough athlete to be on the school's bowling and golf teams. He liked playing Texas Hold 'Em poker, but he never played for much money. Everyone said he was very smart and hung out not with the popular crowd but with the nerdy geeks. "I did hear one person," Hookway said, "who mentioned that in high school, they felt that he felt he was superior to everyone else. And I don't think that he [did, any] more than most people. It's high school. Half the people in the building have a superiority complex."

Hookway did take one extraordinary step, creating a Facebook page he coined "Phil Markoff Is Innocent Until Proven Guilty." The more Hookway gave interviews to the media, the angrier he got that everyone assumed his high school chum was guilty. So he started the page and listed its guiding principle:

Rally against the media who is quick to place blame, against the culture that has forgotten that people like Phil are suspects, not killers . . . [Phil's] guilt or innocence is really not the reason for this group—the reason for this group is encouraging and reminding the American public how our legal system works and to not let them get sucked into the media coverage that is quick to forget the very basis of due process and a fair trial before one's peers.

When asked about the group, Hookway said he wanted to stand by a friend. "I think if everything turns out the worst for Phil, then I can be proud that I at least did everything I could for him," Hookway said. "I wouldn't feel any shame. . . . If things come out for the worst, I know that I can be proud that I've done everything I can do."

Another of Markoff's classmates was John Secord, who moved to Sherrill from California in seventh grade. Like everyone else, he remembers Phil in general terms. It was like Markoff was a ghost—there but not there. "He was one of the first people I met, but I never become super close with him," Secord said. "He was so tall you could spot him from anywhere in middle school. He was always awkward 'cause he was so much taller than everybody else. I don't know, almost like he hadn't grown into his body yet. But he was always a really nice kid. I don't remember him ever being aggressive or mean or anything like that."

Dave Lipke said that Markoff became more introverted as he grew older. "When we were younger, he was a lot more outgoing," he said. "I'm not sure why, what happened like that, but I remember when we were younger . . . he was, like, there for anything. As we got older, he not only kind of grew into more of his own thing but we started talking less and less."

Secord and at least two other high school classmates said Markoff more or less ignored his female classmates, and his guy friends cannot remember him having a single girlfriend. But one girl Markoff did speak to, a classmate named Andrea, said that in all the years she spent with him—from first grade through college—she found him to be "mean, condescending, and arrogant." Andrea said that Markoff enjoyed picking on her and belittling her. "He called me stupid and dumb," she said, "and I really cannot think of one nice thing to say about him."

Even when she was younger and the class was reading *Charlie and the Chocolate Factory*, Andrea remembers Markoff making fun of how long it was taking her to read the book. "His arrogance was his downfall," Andrea said. "He thought his intelligence was a shield and that he was invisible, so I'm not surprised at all by his arrest. He was a mean geek."

She felt so scarred and emotionally bruised by Markoff that she completely avoided him at UAlbany, and said they never exchanged a single word there even though they'd known each other their whole lives. When Andrea heard

Markoff was engaged, she said she was "quite surprised. . . . I could never picture him with a girl. He was just not respectful."

Andrea watched Markoff closely when he appeared on television after his arrest and said his face "looked the same as it did in English class."

Andrea was not the last woman to claim she had problems with Markoff, as everyone would soon hear.

22

College Days

I t's not that Morgan Houston ever *stopped* thinking about Phil Markoff. He was always there in the back of her mind because he was a college friend, a guy from the same frat. They had studied organic chemistry together, sat side by side at lunch, and went out drinking along with their frat brothers and sisters. He's there in all of her graduation photos—good old Phil sitting next to Morgan, both outfitted in cap and gown. In

192 Paul LaRosa and Maria Cramer

February 2009, Morgan sent her old buddy a text: *Happy birthday and congrats on your engagement.* He'd responded in kind and she was planning to send him a longer reply in mid-April when her final exams in podiatry school at Temple University were over. And then . . .

"I logged on to Facebook and a girl that I hadn't talked to in about two years sent me a message saying, 'Oh my God, Morgan.' And I started freaking out because I thought, 'What is this girl going to say to me?' I hadn't talked to her in a while. And she said, 'Have you heard about Phil? Turn on the news. He was arrested as the Craigslist Killer.'"

At that point, Morgan was home in Aiken, South Carolina, a peaceful community in the middle of horse country. What she was hearing was so at odds with the surroundings and what she knew of Phil Markoff that she could scarcely believe it: "I went into shock. I woke up my mother and I started instant messaging [with my friends] and the phone calls were going back and forth. We were all in shock and terrified and in utter disbelief."

Morgan turned on the television and there was Phil. She watched as her college buddy from UAlbany was branded a killer by television news anchors, the police, and Suffolk County district attorney Dan Conley. She saw a video of Markoff in court, looking pretty much as he always had in school, and then the television report flashed the surveillance stills of the tall blond man taken by three hotel security cameras. Morgan felt as thought she'd been punched in the gut. She said she immediately recognized the man in those damning hotel photos as her old schoolmate, "especially the one with the profile; you look at it, and that's Phil. I mean, who knows? Maybe he was there and it wasn't him, and maybe that's not him. But to me, it looked like him in those pictures."

And then Morgan, an attractive brunette, remembered "the incident"—a night in the winter of her sophomore year when she found herself face-to-face with a very different Phil.

"That night," she explained, "a bunch of us had been hanging out. It was probably a little after midnight, and I think Phil and I had been in one cab and other friends were in others. So people get dropped off at different places."

Morgan and Markoff lived in the same high-rise dorm and were dropped off together. Everything was friendly until something came over Markoff. He changed abruptly just before she could slide her key into the front door of the building. "He cornered me and kind of trapped me and pushed me up against the wall and was trying to kiss me. I was turning my head to the side so he couldn't. And I was saying, 'No, Phil. We're just friends. What are you trying to do?' And I was trying to push him away.

"And he was being forceful. I couldn't physically get him off me. He wasn't leaving bruises but I couldn't get him off me. Thankfully, one of my very close friends who also knew him [came] along very shortly after that and he was able to pull him off me. And I was able to escape upstairs. It was in a public area and I'm sure that eventually someone would've come along. But it was very relieving that someone came along so fast, and someone that I knew.

"I felt shocked. I felt a little bit betrayed because I never gave him any signs that he was more than a friend. It wasn't just the two of us out for drinks. A lot of us were out. And I was hurt by it."

Morgan may have been emotionally wounded, but she did not file a report with either the Albany police or campus security. Basically, she gave a friend the benefit of the doubt. "I kind of wanted to forget it," she said. "I knew that he had a lot to drink that night. And I just was trying to chalk it up to that. And he never mentioned it to me. And I didn't see him for a couple of days or a week or so. And I just kind of wanted to forget about it. And I didn't wanna go telling everyone else because I didn't want it to look badly on him."

She forgave but didn't forget what had happened in those few frightful minutes. "I had no control," she said. "I physically couldn't push him away. And anything like that is always . . . it's frightening. Even though it's a friend [you've known] for a while, if you can't push them off you, you don't know how far they're gonna try to go. I don't have experience with anything like this. He wasn't listening to me when I was saying no."

Looking back now, Morgan wonders whether she had glimpsed a secret part of Markoff that evening. "It wasn't the Phil I knew. The Phil I knew was a . . . little bit awkward but a nice, easygoing guy," she said. "I chalked it up to the alcohol. If all of this . . . is proven true, then I should have been a lot more frightened than I was."

Morgan tries not to second-guess herself, but she cannot help replaying the incident again and again in her mind. Did she do the right thing by not reporting him? What would she have said if she had? He was aggressive, but thankfully, nothing had really happened. "I go on a roller coaster of emotions, of one minute thinking the best and one minute the worst, and some minutes I'm frightened and some I'm anxious," she said. "It's not one straight, flat feeling. It's the turmoil of seeing this every time I . . . see his picture. You're still going through shock and it's hard to believe, it's hard to accept. You're still looking back and trying to think of these moments. . . . There had to have been signs. And you're looking for signs in your head. And you're trying to remember. And little things that could have seemed insignificant at the time are starting to seem like they're adding up."

Morgan says she remembers some of Markoff's comments as being a bit out of bounds. "He would be forward with his comments. Sometimes, I'll have a guy friend say, 'Morgan, you look really nice today.' And it just feels nice. But somehow—it's hard to explain— sometimes the way that [Phil] would say it just made me feel a little awkward and uncomfortable. . . . It's so long ago, I can't think of exact words. But I remember him one time complimenting a pair of jeans and saying, 'I love those jeans. You should wear them more often.' But it was just the look that he had on his face when he was saying it that made me feel uncomfortable. And I do have other people compliment me. But I never really get that bad vibe. I just kind of brushed it off as 'It's Phil.' He can be lacking in some social skills. And I just kind of chalked it up to that.

"I thought he was very nice. He was dorky, but so many of us are. I mean, I can be a big dork, too," she said. "So you can't hold that against him, but he was definitely lacking in some social skills. He would make a comment a little bit too late or he would just seem like he [felt] awkward in some situations. It didn't seem like he was always a hundred percent comfortable in his own skin.

"I was never attracted to Phil. I was nice to him, and I thought of him as a friend. I could sometimes get the vibe that he was attracted to me. He would say some things, comments. But I would just kind of brush them off."

Morgan says she never for one moment felt that Markoff was dangerous or psychotic in any way. He seemed worried a lot, but only about his studies. He sometimes spent up to eight hours straight in his room, boning up for a test. "He always did well, and he was intelligent. He was social," she said. "There are degrees of social people within the fraternity. And he wasn't the most social. He wasn't the most charismatic and outgoing. But he wasn't the worst, either. He wasn't a loner. But he also wasn't the life of the party."

Like a few others, Morgan noticed that Markoff did not go out of his way to meet women. She met his fiancée, Megan, only briefly and did not know her well. All three of them had been in the same coed fraternity, but at different times, because Megan was two years older.

James Kehoe ran into Phil Markoff on the UAlbany campus on move-in day back in 2004, when both men were freshmen. He and Markoff were moving into the same dorm at the same time, and it was the type of classic scene played out on thousands of campuses every fall. "He was there with his parents, and everyone seemed perfectly normal. I thought he was smart and friendly," Kehoe said. "And his parents seemed very proud that their son was going to school and getting himself on the track to his career. I'm sure his father was proud of him. He was a dentist, and Phil seemed driven to go into the same field; he wanted to be a doctor."

It was a bright and sunny day, and that's basically the way Kehoe remembers Markoff's personality. "For the most part, he always seemed to have a smile on his face. And just always was willing to talk," Kehoe said.

Both men lived on the same floor—the honors floor. It wasn't exactly *Animal House*, but it did have its moments, and Kehoe said that Markoff shared in the fun. Like everyone else who crossed Markoff's path, Kehoe was bowled over by his friend's intelligence and came to believe that Markoff was one of the most gifted students he'd ever met. If Markoff ever seemed stressed-out—and he did at times—it was only, Kehoe said, because of the heavy workload demanded by a pre-med degree. The stress did not last, at least as far as Kehoe could see. "It never really seemed to get to him that much," he said. "He'd always bounce right back. And after he finished what he had to do, he'd be [his] same old chipper self."

Markoff took a lot of extra courses and graduated in three years, but Kehoe said Markoff never seemed all that different from anyone else. Candid photos of Markoff at college show him posing in silly ways, smiling stupidly for the camera, and yelling boisterously in front of a stack of empty beer cans—pretty standard fare for any college student. No one accused him of being a loner or being weird. He studied a lot, but that's hardly a sign of borderline personality disorder. Classmates say he played a lot of poker and enjoyed it tremendously, but at the same time, they say "So what?" In the years Markoff was an undergraduate, the World Series of Poker in Las Vegas was growing in popularity and became the major television event it is today. Markoff certainly wasn't the only frat guy entertained by a spirited game of Texas Hold 'Em. "The guys in my dorm and all across campus were no different," Kehoe said. "I mean, they'd sit around and they'd have card games. The stakes were low, five dollars here and there. It didn't seem like anything worth being concerned about.

"I know he lost some money, but I don't remember it [being] a lot. He would play to win his money back but it's to be expected. At that time I never really thought of it as any kind of gambling problem. If it did snowball into something like that in the future, that's something that I never got to witness."

Kehoe did notice that Markoff was definitely *not* a ladies' man. "He didn't seem like he ever really gave that much attention to trying to pick up women," Kehoe said. "He was a pretty good-looking guy. He was tall. He was smart. So he was the kind of guy that a lot of girls would go for. And he was a little bit cocky. . . . Not necessarily arrogant. He had that cockiness that girls like. When girls would talk to him, he would just, you know, kind of make jokes and just kind of, you know, have that cocky attitude. He never really gave much back."

If there was one thing that set Markoff apart, it was his politics—he was a die-hard Republican and a member of the College Republicans club on a campus that was mostly made up of Democrats. "We were surrounded by such a left-wing student body, and he was more like me," classmate Jonathan Zierler told *The New York Times*. In 2004, both men journeyed to Washington, DC, with the club to hear speeches by right-wing champions Ann Coulter and Karl Rove. "[Markoff] was a traditionalist as far as things like men's and women's roles in society [go]. He was a throwback to a more conservative era," Zierler said.

That belief in the concept of traditionalism rubbed some the wrong way. Joe Coe spent a lot of time around Markoff in 2007, his final year at Albany. Markoff was friends with one of Coe's suite mates, and spent a lot of time in Coe's living room. Coe, who says he's been openly gay since age thirteen, sometimes found Markoff irritating, and not just because he was always underfoot. "He would say off-color comments about women and oppressed people, which would become an argument with me and other people who lived in the apartment," Coe said.

But like Morgan, Coe was willing to cut Markoff a break. Why? Because Coe thought he was no different from any other straight male on campus. Asked if he thought Markoff was a misogynist, Coe said, "I would say [he was] as much so as most men in our society. There were layers of it. You wouldn't think of him as being a card-carrying member of the KKK. But he was someone who had issues with people of color, had issues with women."

These issues weren't severe enough for Coe to cut Markoff out of his life. In the academic year 2006–2007, Coe saw Markoff regularly, two or three times each week, and his overall impression was that Markoff was Joe College all the way. Coe said Markoff seemed more comfortable in smaller groups, but there were no alarm bells going off in Coe's head. He said that if he had thought Markoff was crazy or weird, he never would have allowed him to hang out in his apartment. Even Markoff's drinking was nothing out of the ordinary, according to Coe. "If you don't like to drink [at UAlbany], you're kind of the exception," he said.

Kehoe ran into Markoff again the year after he graduated, and Markoff was already attending medical school. "It was either at a bar or a party and I was like, 'Hey, Phil. How are you doing? I haven't seen you in a while,' " Kehoe said. "And we just talked for a little bit. I don't really remember much about the interaction other than the fact that it was nice to see him.

I'd never witnessed any kind of disturbing behavior from him. So I don't know how long this reported double life has lasted.

"I pray that this is a case of mistaken identity."

23

Against All Odds

Within days of Phil Markoff's appearance in Boston Municipal Court, *Boston Globe* reporter Maria Cramer received word from her sources that the police had made a preliminary ballistics match between the gun found in Markoff's apartment and the gun used to kill Julissa Brisman. Cramer's sources would not reveal the caliber of the gun, but they said it was *the* most devastating piece of evidence against Markoff.

Private investigator Joe Moura said he thought that Markoff, who loved playing poker, would appreciate the stiff odds he was facing, even though he had not yet been indicted by a grand jury. Of all the evidence, Moura said, "The gun is gonna be number one. If they show that that gun was the gun that was involved in the shooting, you got a 'case closed' situation. See you later. He's gone."

And the gun was only part of the evidence. The police had a lot more: Trisha Leffler's eyewitness identification of Markoff in a photo array; Trisha's underwear allegedly found in his apartment; plastic zip ties similar to those used in the crimes also allegedly found in his apartment; the surveillance photos from both Boston hotels in which the suspect looked very much like him; and the Internet protocol address taken from emails sent by the killer to Julissa Brisman that led investigators to Markoff's doorstep.

Sources speaking to *Globe* reporters added that Markoff's fingerprints were allegedly found on the tape Trisha's assailant had put over her mouth and on the zip ties left at one of the crime scenes. Markoff had not yet been charged in the Rhode Island case but the *Globe* also reported that his fingerprint had been located in the stairway of the Warwick Holiday Inn Express. The security camera photos of that hotel stairway showed a man looking very much like Markoff. In addition, investigators, by tracing Markoff's BlackBerry through cell towers, now knew that he was in the area of the Warwick Holiday Inn at the time of the attack on Amber. "He definitely sent text messages literally within moments of the attack," one official told *Globe* reporter Jonathan Saltzman.

Given the damning nature of the evidence, it was hardly surprising to hear that, within days of his incarceration, Markoff was placed under suicide watch and taken out of the general inmate population at Boston's Nashua Street Jail. Red marks apparently made by shoelaces were reportedly spotted on his neck. Word leaked out that Markoff had been outfitted in what is called a "Ferguson," a heavy smock-type garment designed to prevent the wearer from harming himself. A camera was focused on him twenty-four hours a day. Markoff's lawyer John Salsberg would neither confirm nor deny the suicide story, but he did state the obvious—jail sucked. Of course, he didn't exactly use those words. "I remain very concerned about Philip," Salsberg said. "The transition from being free to being incarcerated is very difficult and I have tremendous confidence that the Suffolk County Sheriff's Department will make sure his safety and well-being are taken care of.

"Keep in mind, he's a young man with no prior record and he's being held in jail. It's difficult for anybody to be there, even if you've been there more than once, but I think he's bearing up."

From the moment he was appointed by the court, John Salsberg kept reporters at arm's length. He made short and sporadic statements, and ignored requests to interview Markoff or his parents. But reporters who covered the courts regularly noted that if anyone could pull a Houdini and get Markoff out from under all the alleged evidence against him, it was Salsberg, a sixty-one-year-old seasoned trial attorney with the unruffled confidence of a veteran litigator. There's no doubt that Markoff was blessed by good fortune when he got Salsberg as his attorney. A graduate of Brandeis University and the New England School of Law, Salsberg teaches at Harvard University, is listed in *Best Lawyers*, and has been dubbed a "Massachusetts Super Lawyer" by *Boston Magazine*. And when anyone remarked upon the uphill fight Salsberg had ahead of him in the Markoff case, someone else would inevitably mention Kyle Bryant.

Kyle Bryant was seventeen years old in September 1999 when he told police in a tape-recorded statement that he was present when his girlfriend—fourteen-year-old Chauntae Jones, who was eight months pregnant at the time—was stabbed, bludgeoned, and buried alive in a shallow grave on the grounds of the former Boston State Hospital in Mattapan. The trial did not take place until 2004, and when it ended, Bryant was found not guilty of murdering Chauntae and her eight-month fetus, which was presumed to be Bryant's unborn child. It remains a stunning verdict because the evidence against Bryant appeared overwhelming. Not only did he admit to being at the scene when Chauntae was buried but the pillowcase found in the grave and the shovel used to bury the teenager were determined to have come from Bryant's home. When the "not guilty" verdict was read after jurors had deliberated for twelve hours over four days, even Bryant's eyes widened in surprise.

The state's theory was that Bryant assisted in killing his onetime girlfriend to avoid being charged with statutory rape against Chauntae, who at the time of her death was an eighth-grade student at St. Mary's Alternative School in Dorchester. In a twenty-five-minute tape-recorded statement that was played to the jury,

Bryant admitted that he knew a hole had been dug for Chauntae at the old hospital to serve as "her final resting place."

On the tape Bryant said that he followed along while his childhood friend Lord Hampton lured Chauntae to the site. Bryant said he did nothing, "like a dummy," while Hampton assaulted Chauntae with unabated fury. He choked her, stabbed her with a six-inch knife, and then beat her with a rock. Bryant said he listened to the mother of his unborn child scream for help but did not help her.

It was a horrific account that the jurors paid close attention to. Then Salsberg called his only witness—Assistant District Attorney David Deakin, who testified that the state had not opened an investigation into the possibility of charging Bryant with statutory rape before the murder. Salsberg claimed that Deakin's testimony proved Bryant had no motive to kill Chauntae. He was facing two counts of murder under case law, which states that all participants in a joint criminal venture are equally culpable—even if only one did the actual killing. In his jury instructions, the judge noted that in order to be found guilty of the "joint venture" charge, jurors had to find that Bryant was present at the scene *and* either shared the intent to murder Chauntae or helped carry out the murder. Salsberg maintained that his client had no idea Lord Hampton planned to kill Chauntae and that he did not participate.

The jury bought Salsberg's argument. When the verdict was read, Chauntae's family was incredulous and court officers had to restrain her mother. "He [Bryant] was as guilty as the other guy," Chauntae's father told the *Globe*. "It was twelve people on the jury that didn't do their part."

Jurors were spirited away from the courthouse for their own safety, but one later called the *Globe* and said, "[Bryant's] being present at the scene was not enough for a joint venture [conviction]." The juror also mentioned that he and others were troubled by the aggressive questioning of Bryant by Detective Dan Keeler, aka Mr. Homicide, who coincidentally was one of the detectives who worked on the Trisha Leffler robbery and kidnapping in the Markoff case.

Salsberg told reporters that he felt for the family of the victim. "I can't forget what happened to Chauntae Jones," he said. "I'll never forget."

Bryant's friend Lord Hampton was tried separately at a later date. Hampton, too, had given police a tape-recorded statement, but he claimed that it was Bryant who stabbed Chauntae after dumping her face-first into the shallow grave, crossing her legs "like a turkey," and then jumping on her back. Hampton admitted to helping pile dirt on the brutalized girl while she was still alive. Hampton was convicted of murder; Bryant walked away a free man.

Of course, the circumstances surrounding the Bryant and Markoff cases are vastly different, but no one in the Boston court system has forgotten the miracle Salsberg pulled off in that case. And Salsberg did make one comment in the Bryant case that resonates for Markoff. "Fortunately for everyone, cases are not decided in the press," he said. "They are only decided by jurors who sit and hear evidence. Unless you're in the courtroom and hear the evidence, you can't pass judgment."

24

Forget About Me

Phil Markoff, who grew up in a two-story colonial house on Thurston Terrace in sedate Sherrill, New York, now calls Boston's Nashua Street Jail home. It's a relatively modern facility that was opened in 1990, replacing the former Charles Street Jail, which dated back to 1851. It is where Markoff's parents now are forced to visit him, and on April 24 his mother, Susan Haynes, and his dad, Dr. Richard Markoff, accompanied by lawyer

John Salsberg, made the trip to see their son for the first time since the arrest. The two of them had said not a quotable word, and it's anyone's guess what they were feeling, but surely it was a painful time. Before the arrest, Markoff must have seemed like a perfect child. Now, if what the police were saying about him was true, he'd brought his family nothing but disgrace.

About twenty members of the press—reporters, producers, and still and video camerapeople—were waiting at the jail's entrance. They shouted questions at Markoff's parents as they made the short walk from a black car to the jail's front door. His parents said not a word, although Salsberg later spoke on their behalf.

The attorney said he wanted to clear up any misunderstandings about why Markoff's parents had waited three days to see him. "He couldn't have any visitors until he was classified by the jail," he said, "and my understanding was that the first day they could come was today. . . . I would just say that everybody who is incarcerated here is in a difficult situation and I wouldn't say [Markoff] is an exception to anyone else here. This is difficult for [his parents]. They really request privacy. They ask that any questions you have, you ask of me. They love their son very much and are supportive of him. That's what they would say if they were speaking to you."

Salsberg said they were very apprehensive about visiting the jail, and when asked what they were afraid of, he was direct: "All of you. . . . In a difficult time, having people from the press put microphones in your face is not something anyone wants."

That visit was soon followed by another from Phil's older brother, Jon, and Jon's wife, Deanna. Within hours, the *Boston Herald* reported that, according to sources, the meeting between the brothers had been emotional and that Markoff had broken down and told Jon, "Forget about me. . . . There is more coming out. . . . Move to California."

When asked about those reported remarks,

Salsberg would neither confirm nor deny what
was said. "Generally speaking, lawyers advise
their clients not to talk about the case," he said.
"What's discussed is typically benign."

There was no way to verify the remarks reported by the *Herald*, but reporters and those
following the case were left to wonder if there
might be other Markoff victims. Had his crime
spree started long before April 10?

25

M4T

If anyone was wondering what Phil Markoff might have meant when he reportedly told his family, "Forget about me.... There is more coming out.... Move to California," one possible answer came days later when NBC reporter Jeff Rossen presented an astounding report on the *Today* show.

A nearly breathless Rossen told viewers that a male "corporate professional" had come forward to reveal that, twice during the previous year, he and Markoff had exchanged erotic emails. This "professional," whose face was covered by shadows to protect his identity, said he had posted a Craigslist ad in the casual encounters section under M4T, which is a catchall term meaning "males seeking to meet transvestites or transsexuals." Markoff answered his ads in 2008 and 2009, and the two began sending a flurry of emails back and forth about what type of sex they enjoyed, and where and when they might meet.

The email exchanges were shown during Rossen's report. Markoff went by the username sexaddict5385 and sent the emails from a Yahoo! account that police confirmed belonged to Markoff. Included in the evidence gathered by police was Markoff's laptop, and sources confirmed to Maria Cramer that the distinctive photograph of a naked torso in those emails was found on Markoff's hard drive. Police have not revealed exactly what else is on Markoff's computer, but if the NBC report is any indication, there may be more evidence that Markoff was attempting to lure men as well as women.

In these emails Markoff sometimes addresses the man as "babe" and under the subject line "hot tongue," Markoff wrote: *I am a 22 y/o grad student. 6'3", 205, good build, blond/blue eyes . . . let me know what else you want to see or know about me . . . what are you into and what are your stats? What are you doing tonight?*

Incredibly, Markoff used his full name (as well as his username), and included photos of his face and torso. Rossen said there were other, X-rated photos that he could not show to early morning viewers. Markoff and his email buddy never met but they exchanged many emails in the spring of 2008, and then again in January 2009, just months before the Craigslist Killer crime spree began.

After Markoff's arrest, the man in shadows heard Markoff's name on TV, went to his Gmail account, and used the search feature. "I typed his name in and it immediately popped right up," he said. "I was scared like you wouldn't believe."

The email with the "hot tongue" subject line was sent on May 2, 2008, less than two weeks before Markoff proposed to Megan McAllister. Rossen asked the man if he thought perhaps he was being set up for a robbery by Markoff. "Honestly, I don't even know," he said.

Was Markoff setting this self-described transvestite up for a robbery? Common sense would indicate otherwise. Markoff had sent a photo of his smiling face as well as given his real name, something police said he did not do with his female victims during the crime spree. If he had, police would not have needed an Internet protocol address or any other virtual fingerprints. They could have just gone to Markoff's apartment and questioned him. Because Markoff included his true identity in the emails sent to the man in shadows, it seems obvious that robbery was *not* Markoff's intent. For his part, the man in shadows said he was very interested in having sex with Markoff. "He seemed like a great guy," he told NBC reporter

Rossen. "He was very cute. I was really taken by his looks."

At the end of the report, Rossen sympathetically wondered aloud to the man what Megan would think when she heard this latest bombshell.

"It would be tough for anyone to hear that [her] fiancé is saying he's single and looking for sex online anonymously with men, men who dress up as women, with transsexuals, with anyone he could get online," the man said. "This person was trolling Craigslist like a Monopoly game."

26

Megan

Megan McAllister is the baby of her
family.

And the McAllisters of Little Sil-
ver, New Jersey, are a very close-knit family.
Megan's parents, Jim and Lynn, have been
married for more than forty years, and they
raised their four children in a loving, nurturing
environment in this suburban community
about forty-five minutes south of Manhattan.
Little Silver, on the banks of the Shrewsbury

River, is every bit the peaceful little town that Sherrill, New York, is, and it's likely that Phil Markoff felt very much at home here whenever he visited Megan's parents.

At twenty-five years old, Megan is not only the youngest member of the McAllister clan but also the only daughter. She has three older brothers who are in their mid-to-late thirties. "She was the baby," says a family friend, Gary.

Gary has known the family for decades and says that Megan was a little more introverted than her brothers, who always tried to protect her. It is no surprise that in a family comprised mostly of men, Megan is particularly close to her mother. "I just remember anytime you saw Megan, her mother was nearby," Gary said. "This family is tight. The values, the morals, and the ethics that come out of that house are something you'd want for your family."

Jim, the patriarch, has always been something of an entrepreneur and has tried his hand at different jobs. He once sold T-shirts, but in recent years, he found a more lucrative line of work selling sheds and swing sets made by the Pennsylvania Amish. "These are not your normal, everyday sheds," Gary said. "They look like little houses. You can put in electric fireplaces and get them refinished. They are actually nicer than some people's homes."

Jim played college basketball, and all three of his sons took up the sport in high school. Megan, too, was athletic and played high school softball, but is plagued by a chronic back condition that has affected her since she was a child.

Family life for the McAllisters sounds almost idyllic. Inside the bilevel home where they've lived for at least twenty years, there is a fireplace, and on the mantel are photographs of all the McAllister children and the five grandchildren. When their kids were young, Jim and Lynn insisted that no matter what activity the boys or Megan had planned, they needed to have a family meal all together at least once a week. Gary says he's read the blogs that question Megan for standing by her man, the posts wondering if she's in denial, but he says that Megan is no fool. She is, he said, just a trusting woman who grew up in a stable home where she was insulated from the worst in people. She did not have a lot of boyfriends when she was growing up, and she put all her trust in Phil. Even detectives trailing the couple before the arrest noticed that the body language between the two seemed a bit one-sided. It seemed to them that she was loving toward him, but he seemed cold toward her.

"When you grow up in a house like that, obviously there shouldn't be any fear," Gary said. "Why did this happen to her? Probably because she's too naive and nice."

Gary said he last saw Megan in December 2008 when her parents threw a holiday party. He visited for only about twenty-five minutes, but he ran across Megan and her oldest brother, Mark. "I asked her, 'So how are you doing?' and she said she was doing great." Megan was beaming and was proud to tell Gary that she was getting married.

He congratulated her, and turned to her brother Mark and joked, "That was quick."

"I know. He's a very nice guy. He's a good guy," Mark said, referring to Phil Markoff.

Gary said he feels bad that such a nice young woman got caught up with a guy who now seems to have been living a secret life. "What a shame that she of all people ended up in this mess," he said. "She was so innocent, a young good kid. You're just happy to see someone like that happy. You're happy to see someone like her be successful. If good things happen to her, you think, 'Good, she's a good kid. She deserves this.' "

In the days following her fiancé's arrest, Megan became a prisoner in her own home. Everyone wanted to know what she was thinking, what it was like to be hoodwinked by someone she trusted and loved so dearly. The press from New York, Philadelphia, and who knows where else descended on her home in force, with remote trucks, video producers, and correspondents. After a few reporters walked up to the door of the family home and asked for a comment, a local police officer politely asked everyone to just wait on the street next to the McAllister house, which is on a corner lot. The weather was beautiful with the sun shining and the temperatures rising into the high seventies, but Megan and her family could not go outside without being swarmed by reporters. All the press could do was hope that someone from the family might say *something*.

Megan was not the only one stuck inside. Her wedding website had listed the names of her bridesmaids, all hometown high school friends who lived nearby. The press knocked on their doors as well, but despite obvious signs that people were home, none would answer her door. A rumor went around that the brides-maids had made a pact not to talk to the press unless Megan gave permission.

In the meantime, the press sat on the curb outside the McAllister home and watched a procession of deliverymen from a nearby store deliver basket after basket, gifts from the anchors of national television shows trying to curry favor with the McAllisters.

What was going through Megan's mind inside that house? One perspective comes from Dr. Michael Welner, clinical associate professor of psychiatry at New York University's School of Medicine. "Think about it," he said. "You've got your whole life wrapped up in someone. Your whole future is invested. It's a belief and a hope that's as intense as a religion. And suddenly to be confronted with the possibility that that's just not real. That that's a fantasy . . . you can't click that off overnight. It's a belief that you organize your life around.

"And then, again, the soul searching. Whom have I picked? Is there something I didn't see? Am I a fool? Can I trust myself? A very difficult and vulnerable place to be. And I absolutely feel for this fiancée.

"[She's asking herself] How did I get involved with a con artist whom I thought was charming? What happens when the person that we love turns out to be someone entirely different? And we find out when it's way too late. What happens when the person we love turns out to be someone we never recognize and we find out way too late?"

Megan wasn't talking, but her father finally did. Jim McAllister walked down the driveway and couldn't help responding to the incessant questions from the press. Asked how his daughter was holding up, he said, "As expected, not well. She's still confident in Phil. Other than that, we are saying a lot of prayers."

Did his daughter have any idea about Markoff's alleged secret life? "Absolutely not," he said, and the short interview was over.

But soon enough, Megan would get a chance to talk to Phil face-to-face.

Megan and Phil

In the twenty-four hours after Phil Markoff was arrested, Megan McAllister was his biggest and most steadfast supporter, sending out those emails stating, among other things, that Markoff was the sort of man who would "not hurt a fly." Bloggers, columnists, and even Barbara Walters and the ladies of *The View* began screaming that Megan was in deep denial and should distance herself from Markoff immediately. But it's not so easy to turn your back on someone you love, and Megan was struggling with a world suddenly turned upside down. After days of staking out Megan's New Jersey home, news crews pulled away to follow other stories, and on April 30, Megan left her home and headed up to Boston for a dramatic face-to-face visit with Markoff, the first time she had seen him since the two were pulled over on I-95 by detectives.

Megan was dressed in a black top and pants and wore giant sunglasses, but it was what she was *not* wearing that caught the attention of the only reporter staked out at the Nashua Street Jail, Eileen Curran of WBZ, the CBS television station in Boston. Curran focused on Megan's ring finger—there was no engagement ring. After being inside for about an hour, Megan and her mother, Lynn, left the jail hand-in-hand and, just as Markoff's parents spoke not a word to the press, neither did Megan or her mother.

But Megan had retained a New Jersey attorney, Robert Honecker, to be her conduit to the press, and he *did* stop and speak to Curran.

"She's been distraught at coming up and meeting with him," said Honecker. "She feels good about seeing him, but now it's time to get on with other things in her life. They met and spoke for a significant amount of time, and she was emotional. She a bright, articulate, strong young woman and beginning to understand that she needs to find strength from those around her and take care of herself and the rest of her life. This was a big step for her to realize the seriousness of the charges that her fiancé faces and to get on with her life."

Honecker said Megan had not spoken to the grand jury hearing evidence on the case, but was ready to cooperate. "I know that we're going back to New Jersey," he said. "She will take up her life back in New Jersey with family and friends . . . and unless requested by the district attorney, I don't expect her to return to Boston to see [Markoff]. . . . You have a young woman whose dreams of a life to be are no longer there. She's going to be taking it one day at a time."

Megan's attorney said she would move back in with her parents and resume classes in the fall. Various media outlets reported that Megan would attend an offshore medical school on the Caribbean island of St. Kitts, but that could not be confirmed. Honecker had mentioned that there were two reasons for Megan to go to Boston. One, obviously, was to see Markoff. The other was to pick up some items from the Highpoint apartment. By then, an eviction notice was on the door of their third-floor apartment.

Megan herself issued a statement to the press:

In the past two short weeks, my life and what I hoped my life to be has dramatically changed. I want to thank my family and my friends who have supported me during this very difficult time. Without them, I do not know how I could make it through this nightmare. I hope they know that I love each and every one of them.

I also love my fiancé and I will continue

to support him throughout this legal process. My heart goes out to all of those afflicted by these events, especially the families and individuals who have personally suffered from this tragedy.

It is my intent to fully cooperate with my fiancé's attorney as well as the Suffolk County District Attorney's Office as they both continue their investigations. I can only tell them what I know and what is the truth. I will expect that these discussions will occur within the next several days.

What has been portrayed and leaked to the media is not the Philip Markoff that I know. To me and my family, he is a loving and caring person, and in the eyes of the law and constitution, he is innocent until proven guilty beyond a reasonable doubt. I just can only hope that the criminal justice system will not be overwhelmed and persuaded by what is being put forth in the media. My fiancé's fate should not rest in the court of public opinion, but rather in a court of law.

When asked about the impending August wedding, Honecker told reporters, "The wedding . . . is off and being dismantled. Any chances for that event to occur in the future I would suggest would be unlikely. It has been a traumatic and emotional time for this strong young woman, but she's beginning to come back."

No more confirmation was needed, but William Forte of the B-Street Band, the Springsteen tribute band booked for the Markoff-McAllister wedding, announced that he had received an email from a member of Megan's family telling him "there was no way the wedding was going to happen in August."

Forte said that, under the circumstances, he was returning Megan's $500 deposit. "They're very distraught," he said of the family. "They're trying to protect their daughter. I think it's only natural."

28

Medical School

If Phil Markoff is indeed the Craigslist Killer, then he's a genius at time management. If the allegations are true, then he planned and carried out a series of violent crimes in two states, regularly made the long drive—two hours each way—from Boston to Connecticut to gamble at Foxwoods casino, *and* still managed to be a "fantastic" student at one of the most prestigious and demanding medical schools in the country. And let's not forget that, at least in theory, he was helping to plan a wedding. Whatever else you say about the Craigslist Killer, he never looked a bit harried at the hotels where he was photographed. While he may have been driven by inner demons, the killer managed to look almost blasé, even after shooting a woman in a hotel doorway at point-blank range.

The moment it was revealed that Markoff was a second-year medical student at Boston University School of Medicine, administrators went into protective mode. Dr. Karen Antman, the medical school dean, sent out an email to students that basically warned them to shut up: *You may be privy to personal information on this student through social media networking sites and other technologies. Please use caution and discretion in discussing this case on those sites . . .*

The email had its intended effect. Students scurried away from reporters, saying that medical school was so competitive that they did not want their names associated with a potential killer. A couple of professors said Markoff's involvement was a shock because he was such a "fantastic" student. And a poster on a national online forum used by medical students warned everyone to be sensitive in their remarks, as "it's not an easy time for us at BU right now."

As reporters dug in and contacted virtually everyone who had had anything to do with Markoff over his short life—whether it was in his hometown, at his college, at his residence, or at BU's medical school—people professed to know *of* him but not really to *know* him. No one claimed to be, or was identified as, a good friend.

One of the few medical school classmates to speak of Markoff was Tiffany Montgomery, a woman who describes herself as Markoff's former lab partner at BU. Montgomery said she dropped out of school because of financial problems. Given the reticence of most people to say anything about Markoff, Tiffany's comments to a *Boston Globe* reporter seemed refreshingly frank. She said she was "not even remotely surprised" that Markoff turned out to be the Craigslist Killer.

"He just wasn't right in the head, and I knew it," said Montgomery, twenty-six, who said she spent hours with Markoff each day in the lab. She said others in the lab confided in her that they, too, felt that way.

"I got the impression that he was really disturbed. . . . One day, he'd be warm and friendly and smiling, and the next day you'd see him and the clouds had rolled in. And you'd say to yourself, 'This is the fifty percent of the week when it's the upset, brooding Phil, and not the smiling happy Phil.'"

Tiffany considered telling school authorities that he might be suicidal, but never did.

Another of Markoff's classmates, Joseph, said, "To be perfectly honest, Phil came off as arrogant to me. He didn't seem like a person I wanted to get to know. There are a few people in the class who are just loners. I'm sure there are some that I've never spoken to or that hardly anyone knows. When you have a hundred and seventy-five-ish [sic] students, you're going to get a spectrum of people from very outgoing to nearly invisible. When [Markoff] did come to class last year, he sat a few rows back from the front. I also saw him a few times during class-sponsored events at bars and clubs. His actions didn't stick out. Like everyone else, he had a drink in his hand and was talking to classmates. I don't know any of his friends and I have no idea who he hung out with."

But Joseph did provide a valuable insider's look into what attending BU medical school is like. "Medical school is high-tech," he explained. "BU videotapes all of its lectures and therefore does not require the students to actually come to class specifically for lecture. However, they are required to complete tests, do clinical work, meet in small groups, and participate in anatomy lab. At first, students came to class often. By the time the second semester of classes started, fewer people [showed] up to lecture. During the second year, there are no formal lab classes—it is mostly self-learning and lectures. Therefore, fewer and fewer people came to class. By the second semester of the second year, you'd be lucky if half the class showed up.

"Our school supports independent learning. It does *not* mean that we're a lazy bunch. I'd say that the coursework of second year is much more demanding than [that of] the first year, and it forces students to manage their time efficiently."

One reason Markoff appeared to have so much leisure time is because he most likely did a lot of studying on his own and rarely traveled to the campus—just like everyone else. "Not coming to class is common," Joseph said. "I personally found it much more convenient and efficient to watch lectures back to back to back at home or at a café and *not* commute to school. . . . I didn't see [Markoff] often. Maybe half a dozen times at most this entire year, and those meetings were required.

"If I had to guess, [I'd say] Phil probably did what a lot of other people in class do—sleep in, read notes all day long, and then watch the lectures if he wanted to or if he had time to,"

Joseph said. "Tests were every two to three weeks (sometimes longer), and small group meetings happened every week to two weeks on average. My guess is that he was actually on campus no more than once or twice a week. Three times at the most. He would have had plenty of time to drive to wherever he wanted. I had a friend who flew back to California for a week during class. I often made time to do some personal projects. We students have mastered the art of time management. He's obviously a bright guy and it probably wasn't difficult for him to juggle it all."

Of course, there were some classes, such as anatomy, that Markoff had to attend in person. Tiffany Montgomery was Markoff's lab partner in that class, but the anatomy lab was during the first year, and if the police are correct, we all know how Markoff allegedly repurposed his copy of *Gray's Anatomy*.

Joseph said that, while medical school is rigorous, getting passing grades is not as demanding as an outsider might expect: "All you have to do is pass the exam and you're good. I knew people who tried their hardest to get the best grades they could, even though it still means they're just passing. I knew others who didn't care what they got as long as they passed. If you're shooting to just pass, then you'll most likely have more time on your hands. This sounds like bad form, but the grades from the first two years of school don't particularly matter for landing a good residency. It is much more important to do better during the clerkship years, one's third and fourth year of medical school. That takes the pressure off of us a little bit during the first two years."

In the aftermath of Markoff's arrest, some have questioned what type of psychological testing is done by BU School of Medicine. The answer is none at all, according to a school spokeswoman. This is not unusual. According to the Association of American Medical Colleges, none of their members do specific psychological screening. Unless an issue such as a family suicide or a history of depression arises during the initial interview, the applicant's psychological history is not something that is routinely discussed. And Markoff in nearly every way must have seemed like a perfect med school candidate—he had the grades, even, as his classmate Tiffany describes, "an uncommon mind." His father was a dentist. The healing arts were in the family. What was there not to like?

Rachel K. Sobel, a doctor who writes for *The Philadelphia Inquirer*, addressed this issue in a column about Markoff titled "Scrubbing In: Keeping the Unfit out of Medicine." Medical schools, she wrote, have rigorous requirements that consider the character of the applicant, but these standards may still miss underlying psychological issues.

Medical schools look for people who are well-rounded, accomplished in more than just school. They want to know about leadership ability and initiative. They want to train doctors with good character traits. So admissions officers ask for essays and recommendations, and conduct live interviews.

These no doubt screen out the vast majority of sociopaths. But the interesting thing is: This is the last time until a doctor does something really bad that he or she is kept out of the profession. And these barriers aren't that hard to hurdle.

One-hour interviews and a one-page statement can reveal only so much. Recommendations can gloss over character defects. A teacher may feel obliged to back a student even if there are doubts.

Then, once admitted to medical school, it's almost impossible to get kicked out. The old joke—"What do you call the person who graduated last in his class from medical school? Doctor"—certainly resonates here.

Incredibly, this is not the first time that a student attending BU School of Medicine stands accused of being a killer. In March 2001, Daniel Mason, a fourth-year BU medical student, went on a murderous rampage of his own. Mason was getting close to graduation—finally. It had taken him nearly seven years to finish, instead of the normal four, because he reportedly failed several medical clerkships.

In Mason's case, there were warning signs. In fact, if BU had done a criminal records check on Mason, it would have discovered his past, and might have thought twice about admitting him. (Three years ago, BU instituted criminal checks for its medical school applicants.) The first incident dates to 1988 when, while attending Dartmouth College, he got into a minor dispute over weights at a gym. He was arrested but not convicted in that instance and agreed to undergo psychological testing. He graduated from Dartmouth in 1993, and that year was arrested a second time for breaking into a girlfriend's house and allegedly threatening to murder her. More psychological testing followed.

Soon after, he was admitted to BU School of Medicine. His life was comparatively quiet until 1997, when he got into a life-changing argument with Russian immigrant Gene Yazgur over a parking spot. Apparently, the moving truck Yazgur was driving was blocking Mason's car. Yazgur asked Mason to wait five minutes but he refused. Instead, Mason tried to move the truck himself, and when Yazgur objected, Mason attacked him with a knife and nearly took off his ear. Mason was convicted of assault, placed on probation, and continued his studies. Again, it's unclear if BU had any knowledge of his crime.

But Yazgur could not forget it. He sued Mason and in 2001 won a civil judgment that required Mason to pay $118,000 over a twenty-year span. Mason, a former commando in the Israeli army who owned a 9mm shotgun, was incensed and told Yazgur, "You'll never see a penny of that money."

On March 1, 2001, Mason received a notice from the Sheriff's Department ordering him to begin making the payments. Mason had another idea. The following night, he climbed into Yazgur's bedroom at 5:30 a.m. and shot him in the chin. Yazgur woke up and tried to escape, but Mason shot him five more times, shattering both his legs. He then shot and killed Yazgur's roommate, Michael Lenz, twenty-five, and pumped five bullets into Yazgur's dog, Sampson, who died at his master's feet. Yazgur survived and called 911 before lapsing into a coma. He eventually underwent nearly two dozen operations and said the shooting nearly destroyed his life. His murdered roommate, Lenz, a Minnesota native, was said to be a lovely and gentle man who liked to write poetry.

Within days, Mason, who had escaped from the scene of the crime, was arrested at the Boston Medical Center while wearing green scrubs and a white lab coat. He was two months away from getting his MD degree, and the day after his arrest, he was scheduled to begin a pediatrics rotation at North Shore Children's Hospital.

Instead, he was convicted of murder and received two life sentences from Judge Christine McEvoy, who told Mason: "You are a destroyer and an executioner, a cruel and vicious person."

29

Craigslist Under Fire

C raig Newmark, the Craig behind Craigslist, has told interviewers that his corporate mantra and guiding philosophy is to "give people a break," and that's why—in the vast majority of cases—he does not charge for placing ads on his website. "We're about restoring the human voice to the Internet," Newmark told the *Los Angeles Times* a few years back.

But once it was revealed that the Craigslist

Killer had picked his victims off Craig's famous list, no one seemed willing to give Newmark a break.

"When I learned about this killing [of Julissa Brisman], it tragically confirmed what I knew from other incidents," said Richard Blumenthal, the attorney general of Connecticut. "This brutal, heinous crime is simply the tip of the iceberg in terms of criminal activity that can result from Craigslist ads for prostitution and pornography. And that is the reason that law enforcement officials . . . are so focused on trying to make this site, and the Internet, safer."

Others were even more vociferous, especially Chicago's Cook County sheriff, Tom Dart, who's made a habit of attacking Craigslist. In early March 2009—well before Trisha Leffler visited Boston—Dart said, "Craigslist is the single largest source of prostitution in the nation."

He's right about one thing—Craigslist is big. It is the seventh most visited website in the

United States with 10 billion page views per month, according to Craigslist CEO Jim Buckmaster. The site may have its critics, but it also has a lot of fans; many people love Craigslist and visit it nearly every day. It's easy to use, has a certain stripped-down, ugly-but-pretty charm, and best of all, it's free. At least, it's free to the vast majority of the 25 million people who use it each month. The site charges only for job listings in ten United States cities, for New York brokers who run apartment ads, and for those who advertise in the former erotic services section—which was renamed "adult services" in the aftermath of the Craigslist Killer controversy. The company has said it donates all the profits it receives from its erotic ads. Critics say that hardly matters since Craigslist profits from erotic ads in other ways, namely the tremendous traffic such ads drive to the site.

Blumenthal says that Craigslist presents a unique opportunity for law enforcement. "If we can make an example of Craigslist and use it as a model with their cooperation, it will send a very powerful message to other sites," he said. "Not just ads or classifieds but all of the social networking and other sites on the Internet to make them safer. Our goal as law enforcement officials is not just to prosecute crime but to prevent it. And what better way to reach people and safeguard them than to make these sites safer?

"Craigslist has the means and a moral obligation, a real responsibility, to make this site safer. Like any bricks-and-mortar establishment, Craigslist has a responsibility to keep its customers safe. And even though it may be a virtual reality, it still has that real obligation.

"Prostitution is not a victimless crime. And people should understand that what happened in Boston is only the tip of the iceberg. There is human trafficking, child exploitation, illicit drug activity, all associated with these kinds of ads because the bottom of the iceberg is much, much bigger than anyone understands."

All this criticism raining down on Craig

Newmark's beleaguered head comes in spite of his making an agreement in the fall of 2008 with some forty attorneys general nationwide. In that agreement, Newmark promised that his company would require a phone number and credit card from everyone placing ads in the website's erotic services section.

Blumenthal says that now is the time for Craigslist to do even more. "The Markoff case has captured the imagination of Connecticut and the country in a way that is very unique and offers a unique opportunity to pressure Craigslist, or perhaps persuade them is a more polite term, to do the right thing," he said. "Adopt these measures like new blocking technologies, rewards for reporting wrongdoings, penalties for rule breaking, and screenings that prevent these ads for prostitution and pornography."

What is going on here is a cultural and philosophical clash between the opinions of old-time law-and-order types like Sheriff Dart, and the belief in free and open communication on the Internet that is espoused by Newmark and Buckmaster. Parry Aftab, an Internet privacy and security lawyer for WiredSafety, the world's largest and oldest cyber safety organization, said Newmark and Buckmaster "are old-time Internet. . . . They believe that anybody who wants to communicate things using technology should be able to do it. So it's a lot of free-speech issues, which I know are important to them."

Craig Newmark is an interesting figure who began his site back in 1995 in what might be considered the Paleolithic era of the Internet. Newmark, a fifty-six-year-old former New Jersey resident and shy techno nerd, holds a computer science degree from Case Western Reserve University in Cleveland, Ohio. He made his way west and put in years at some large computer companies before beginning an email list in the mid-1990s to help those in San Francisco find technology jobs. As the email list grew, Newmark began posting the job listings on his own website, and invited others to add to his list. People starting posting about everything imaginable, and Craigslist became what it is today. Its graphic design, or lack thereof, has not changed in a significant way. The peace sign remains the company logo. It is the classic viral Internet story.

No one could have predicted that the site— "a happy accident," as Newmark calls it— would grow into the behemoth it is today. In 2009, it was estimated that Craigslist generated more than $100 million in revenue, according to a study done by Classified Intelligence, part of the AIM Group, a media and consultant firm in Orlando, Florida. Consider that in 2004, the site generated only $9 million. The astonishing leap in Craigslist's fortunes has coincided with the incredible drop in newspaper classified advertising, and many feel that there is a direct correlation between the two figures. Indeed, some have said that the only thing Craigslist is guilty of killing are newspapers.

Perhaps even more impressive is that Craig Newmark, a portly fellow with a trademark goatee and glasses, who has joked in the past about his inability to attract women, has built his empire on his terms, never straying from his populist roots. He has a self-deprecating sense of humor and often refers to himself as "the Forrest Gump of the Internet." As of 2009, Craigslist still has only thirty employees, who work out of a Victorian house in San Francisco, the site's original home base. Newmark himself answers the phone and sometimes makes calls to those he feels are abusing the site, like New York Realtors who occasionally try to skirt Newmark's rules. He lives relatively modestly, taking a reported $200,000 annual salary, and has simple tastes. He was raised Jewish but says that the music and poetry of Leonard Cohen "is the closest thing I have to prayer."

Most of those who post on Craigslist are provided with anonymous email addresses, which might give some users the mistaken impression that they are completely anonymous. As discussed earlier, one's Internet protocol address is still traceable, and Craigslist knows a poster's correct email address. But people remain unaware. "I think it's just that we're seeing a growing trend of adults who are getting into trouble online," Aftab said.

Overwhelmingly, the transactions on Craigslist are routine, and the site works because it brings people together in ways that are beneficial to both sides. Aftab said that the bad results that do sometimes derive from the site could be avoided if people would just "engage their brains."

What critics like Dart, Blumenthal, and others want from Craigslist is better monitoring of their adult and erotic ads. But the free-wheeling Newmark and Buckmaster bristle at the idea of exerting more control over their users. Newmark and his band of merry men in San Francisco already spend most of their time monitoring the website. Moreover, the Craigslist brain trust says its 25 million users regularly monitor the site for scams and objectionable postings. It's simple to "flag" an ad that seems like it might be a scam, or be illegal or racist. If the ad is flagged by a certain number of people, it is automatically removed from the site.

It is Newmark and Buckmaster's contention that no one can do a better job of monitoring the site than all those users. "If you look at the data on sites, large and small," Buckmaster said, "you'll find that sites that attempt to police their users and postings, using staff who are reviewing postings—it doesn't matter if they have hundreds or if they have thousands or if they have tens of thousands of staff—can't do nearly as good a job as tens of millions of users who are empowered to remove each and every listing on the site."

And he points out that Craigslist cooperates with the authorities when asked for help in nabbing criminals. "When it comes to working with law enforcement, our emphasis is on a rapid turnaround of any inquiry they may have for us," said Buckmaster. "We want to get them the information . . . that they need to solve these crimes."

"They run around acting as if they should

be given a citizen award because they cooperate with law enforcement," Dart said. "I believe we all should cooperate with law enforcement when we're involved with a crime. I don't think it's something you should get a pat on the back for. They keep harping on the fact that, well, this is a self-monitored site. And we're against crime. Wow. Fantastic. You're against crime. So am I. I'm doing something about it. You're doing nothing."

Sheriff Dart said he is not arguing that this country's rampant underground black market in prostitution is the fault of Craigslist. "Prostitution's been around forever. Being robbed, assaulted, killed—that's been around for a long time," he said. "The thing here, though, and it's abundantly clear, [is that] if you are somebody who's looking to harm a prostitute, to rob a prostitute, boy, your road map's right here.

"You go to the Internet. You get on there. One mouse click away, you have somebody who in the ad has identified that they're an independent contractor. They have nobody that they're connected with. They've said that they'll do outcalls, meaning they'll show up at any location you name. What more would some twisted person who wants to harm these people need?"

His point, Dart said, is that the Internet generally, and Craigslist specifically, has made picking out victims a very easy thing to do. "Frankly, from talking to the prostitutes, it's abundantly clear that their site of choice is Craigslist," said Sheriff Dart. "The number one site that we have come across, that everybody else has come across when they deal with prostitution on the Internet has been Craigslist."

Trisha Leffler does not disagree. When asked why she used Craigslist to post her ads, she said, "It's really easy to use and you get a great response. It's very lively."

But if it's a great site for prostitutes, it's also a great site for anyone targeting them, Dart maintains.

Buckmaster—the public voice during this controversy, as the shy Newmark has stayed tucked away back in San Francisco—was no doubt feeling the pressure from the legal community and newspaper reporters when he made one surprising misstep during the Craigslist Killer controversy. He sent an email to the *Boston Globe* in which he stated: "I would not describe any section of our site as 'sex-related.'"

Even defenders of the way Craigslist does business had to laugh at that one. All anyone needs to do, even today, is to look at what is listed under the adult services section. There are hundreds, sometimes thousands, of ads showing women in skimpy bikinis, offering sensual massages. You don't need to "engage your brain" very much to understand what these women are offering.

The point that Buckmaster comes back to again and again is that if you commit a crime using Craigslist as your source, you will be caught. "One thing you notice in virtually every story you read about a crime occurring on Craigslist," he said, "[is that] they all have the same ending. . . . Namely, that the person who commits the crime is apprehended and put behind bars. I think it's slowly getting out. . . . Criminals aren't necessarily the brightest people. But, it is slowly getting out to them that if they use Craigslist to commit a crime, they are going to be caught, because they inevitably create an electronic trail to themselves that law enforcement can easily follow."

Indeed, it's not known exactly what role Craigslist played in helping investigators track Phil Markoff, but Attorney General Blumenthal has said publicly that the website did lend its expertise in the case. And once Craigslist puts its resources behind tracking someone's online activity, it can do quite a lot. That was clear in the case of Michael Anderson, a nineteen-year-old who murdered Katherine Ann Olson, a twenty-four-year-old college graduate who offered her services as a nanny on Craigslist in 2007. Anderson, pretending he wanted to hire Olson, lured the young woman to his parents' home in Minneapolis, where he shot her in the back with a .357 Magnum before dumping her body in the trunk of her car and leaving her to die.

Newmark was horrified. He bonded with Olson's family and told them he'd help in any way he could. He even took the unprecedented step of attending the young woman's memorial service. But that wasn't all. To help the police and the prosecution, Newmark ordered up a 127-page three-ring binder detailing every time Anderson ever used the site, whether it was clicking on a link, posting an ad, or answering someone else's. Newmark also sent customer service representative Clint Powell to Anderson's murder trial, where Powell testified about Anderson's usage. The young man had begun surfing Craigslist in innocent ways, selling ice-fishing equipment, *Star Trek* figurines, and stereo equipment. But in October 2007, the month Olson was murdered, Anderson's activity on the site shifted to women. He advertised that he was looking for an NSA (no strings attached) relationship or women who would pose in videos or model bathing suits. He also began monitoring ads for babysitters, which is where he found Olson. Anderson was convicted of Olson's murder and is now serving a life sentence. Well before Philip Markoff was arrested, Anderson was the original Craigslist Killer.

And if Craigslist compiled that type of dossier on Anderson, one can only imagine what will turn up when they turn the spotlight on Markoff. When and if Markoff goes to trial, a Craigslist company representative most likely will be among the witnesses.

30

Phil's Secret Life

In 2008 Sony Pictures Classics released the film *Married Life*, a period piece set in the late 1940s that starred Pierce Brosnan, Chris Cooper, Rachel McAdams, and Patricia Clarkson. The characters are good-hearted people and upstanding citizens who nonetheless cheat on and betray their partners in a variety of duplicitous ways until the movie ends with these words uttered by Pierce Brosnan's character, Richard Langley: "If you think you know what the person sleeping next to you is thinking, think again."

Megan McAllister could relate to those sentiments. And the film suggests that all of us can, because ultimately, it may be impossible to know what's going through someone's mind, even someone you think you know intimately. According to her father and the police, Megan had no idea what Markoff was up to, and she had been dating and living with him for three years.

But Markoff clearly was up to *something*. When he allegedly warned his family in a jailhouse conversation that more information was coming out, everyone wondered if he had brutalized other women. But when a transvestite went public to reveal embarrassing details about Markoff's desire for kinky sex, reporters began to wonder if Markoff's real warning was of the possible discovery of a secret online life.

By plugging Markoff's acknowledged Yahoo! username sexaddict5385 into various search engines, law enforcement officials and reporters began to uncover some interesting results. The first item to pop up was an online profile at Passion.com under the same username, with the same torso shot cops found on Markoff's computer. Passion.com, which bills itself as *Sexy personals for passionate singles*, is one of a handful of sexually explicit dating websites under the umbrella of AdultFriendFinder.com. The Passion.com site is filled with provocative photos of scantily dressed men and women. Like many of the AdultFriendFinder.com sites, Passion.com is, to say the least, titillating. By tracing Markoff's usage on the site, it appears he used it to read and comment on various sexually explicit articles. For instance, he posted a comment on how much he enjoyed an article by a sex worker who drew comparisons between her job and a one-night stand.

The discovery of the apparent Markoff profile on Passion.com was no doubt embarrassing to Markoff, but the web does draw people in, and if Markoff enjoyed a little online pornography, he was hardly alone. AdultFriendFinder.com claims to have 32 million members worldwide and was purchased by the Penthouse Media Group in 2007 for $500 million.

After discovering Markoff's Passion.com profile, Steve Huff, a veteran true-crime blogger who runs the True Crime Report website under the auspices of Village Voice Media, got a tip. It was suggested that if he added an 8 to Markoff's username, making it sexaddict53885, he would find a lot more. Huff did, and these results went well beyond that initial profile. Huff discovered that Markoff apparently had posted several other profiles of himself on Alt.com, Extreme Restraints, and GayClubList. GayClubList bills itself as *Your Worldwide Gay & Lesbian Resource*, while ExtremeRestraints.com says it is *The Ultimate Fetish Store*. Alt.com bills itself as the world's largest adult personal site for those interested in bondage and many other alternative lifestyles. On all three sites, Markoff included the same torso photograph that he sent with his real name and a head shot to the transvestite in the NBC report. And the profile on Alt.com, created in May 2007, gives telltale identifying characteristics, including the fact that the user is a graduate student in Boston, is six foot three, has blond hair and blue eyes, and shares Markoff's birthday, February 12, 1986. And that wasn't all. On this site, Markoff stated that, sexually, he is interested in "email exchange, phone fantasies . . . and active participation" with men, women, transvestites, transsexuals, and those who are transgender.

Online, his sexual life was anything but plain vanilla; he expressed an interest in bondage, oral and anal sex, and any number of other fetishes—as long as he could play the role of a "submissive." He had twelve virtual "friends" on the site, including one with the name XtremeDomme and another, a woman, who wrote that she desired a "submissive male to serve me." There was also a man who claimed to be a gay firefighter looking for a "submissive boy . . . could that be you?"

The Boston Police investigators, who are in possession of Markoff's laptop, are aware of

Markoff's online sex life and are investigating it. But Markoff's prurient sexual interests are a side issue for the cops unless it leads to more victims—men, women, or transgendered.

Because of the surreptitious nature of these relationships, it is nearly impossible to verify independently if Markoff acted on his desires. The only possible clue comes from one persistent poster on Huff's True Crime Report website, who contends that he repeatedly spotted Markoff at a known gay cruising spot in Boston. In one of a half-dozen posts, the tipster writes:

> Many guys . . . know him by face and recognize his pictures. The problem is that no one wants to speak out . . . he [Markoff] would lure men to the bathroom by placing ads on the web for a particular time and day, and middle aged straight men from all over town would come . . . . He was always on his messenger hooking up with his next batch. There was always a weirder than

weird air about him, and some days he was actually quite moody. It's not clear that he wasn't getting money from these guys.

It's difficult to verify this story because the poster would not correspond privately and would not answer some specific questions. But the postings are written in a very credible and straightforward way and they do not sound so far-fetched when one considers them in the context of the NBC report, the Alt.com profile (where Markoff expresses a desire to engage in sex and bondage with women, men, transvestites, and transsexuals), and Markoff's alleged statement warning his family to move to California because there was more damning information coming out.

The larger question is what, if anything, all of this online sexual activity had to do with Markoff's seven-day crime spree, and the answer may be . . . nothing at all. Stephen Elliott is a thirty-six-year-old well-regarded memoirist and political activist from San Francisco who is an active participant in the S&M and fetish world. In several of his seven books—including the provocatively titled *My Girlfriend Comes to the City and Beats Me Up*—Elliott writes of his own sexual proclivities in the world that he calls "my community." He is up front about being a submissive who enjoys bondage and sex in many forms. "Transvestite sex is so common," he said. "I've had sex with people who are transgendered and I still get up to go to work in the morning. It doesn't mean you can't function or you're a total freak."

Indeed, there is nothing in Elliott's appearance that would suggest he is anything other than a gifted writer and part-time writing instructor at Stanford University. It is only when you read his books—his latest is *The Adderall Diaries: A Memoir of Moods, Masochism and Murder*—that you become aware that there is a lot going on under the surface, much of it involving sexual activity that a lot of Americans would consider extreme. He contends that nothing criminal can be inferred from Markoff's apparent secret sexual life. "Having a secret life has no connection to Markoff being a murderer. It's more of a coincidence than a connection," he said.

"You never know about a person's relationship to money and sex. All of sex is weird. We don't think it's weird when someone has a preference for a blonde because it's the majority but it's still a fetish. Because bondage is in the minority, we make it out to be strange. A lot of people are into it—it's not really that unusual—but they don't want to admit what they're into because of what people will think of them."

Elliott believes that the Craigslist Killer's motives—indeed anyone's motives—are simply unknowable. To Elliott, it is a fool's quest, and it's interesting to note that the law is on his side—district attorneys do not have to prove motive in a criminal case. "The quickest way to be wrong about anybody is to say you understand their motives," Elliott said. "Motives are incredibly complicated. People do things for a thousand different reasons—the weather, the sugar they had in the morning—it's a culmination of events. We always want to say 'He did it because . . .' But the moment someone says they know why someone did something is the moment they're wrong. I know they're wrong, and so does the person they're talking about.

"Obviously the Craigslist Killer is a monster, but the fact that he may be into S&M is not that unusual," Elliott said. "The percentage of killers [with an interest in] S&M is the same as the [percentage] of people into it in the general population. The same as the percentage of any group whether they are Muslim, Christian fundamentalist, whatever. . . . There is no link between his proclivity for S&M and the fact of him being a murderer."

But Dr. Michael Welner, a clinical associate professor of psychiatry at New York University's School of Medicine, said that Markoff's secret life may indeed have had something to do with his alleged crimes, but not because of his predilection for bondage or bisexuality. What may have made Markoff a killer was his desire to keep that part of his life secret. "Nobody is more invested in anonymity than someone with a secret sexual orientation," Welner said.

Welner is a well-respected figure in the psychiatric community and is founder and chairman of a group of forensic scientists who call themselves the Forensic Panel. From the moment Markoff was arrested, Welner has maintained that Markoff was not living a double life so much as a secret life. "As a forensic psychiatrist . . . I see a person who has a full-time life as a medical student, is absorbed in a relationship and engaged to be married and someone whose criminal record is nonexistent as far as public record before April 10," he said. "And then, beginning April 10 and continuing for seven days, he commits three serious crimes. That's a crime spree. And crime sprees don't reflect a double life.

"Crime sprees reflect a sudden change in a person—a significant event going on in their lives where they become unhinged and make a lot of bad choices that can be destructive."

The question Welner poses is *why* Markoff allegedly did what he did when he did it. Why did his alleged spree begin April 10 and not six months before or six months after? "The most important missing piece in this equation is: What was the event, the trigger, the threshold that saw Markoff cross from a life totally indistinguishable from any medical student, any of his peers, into one that we're talking about as shocking?"

Given Markoff's secret sexual life, Welner speculated on a couple of possibilities. Maybe someone discovered Markoff's secrets and was attempting to blackmail him. That would account for why he suddenly needed money. Or it could be that someone, perhaps in a known gay cruising spot, recognized him. The idea that Markoff may have been on the verge of being unmasked, along with the pressure of his impending nuptials that required him to pretend he was a happy heterosexual, may have been enough to unglue him. Perhaps he wanted to escape the life he'd constructed for himself and wanted to jump off the marriage train before it was too late. "Secrets are things that nobody knows about except ourselves," Welner said. "Our sexuality. *Our real sexuality*. The things that really cause us pain. Our sensitive spots and what we're frightened about. How open are all of us? How open are each of us about all of those things? Psychiatry teaches me that we are not.

"For some people, those secrets are catastrophic. And for some people, those dark secrets will present us with a fork in the road where we make wrong, bad choices. . . . I see Markoff that way," he said. "Something in his secrets took him to a fork in the road where he made a choice that he couldn't keep private. And that he couldn't push away. And that, sadly, destroyed at least one other person."

Welner does not claim to know what triggered Markoff's sudden and alleged change in behavior, but he believes something caused him to snap. "It was a personal crisis," he said.

"Something that shakes you to your core. Is it your future because of your career? Is it your future because of money? Is it your future because you're going to be exposed? Can't guess. He'll take us there. The evidence will take us there.

"If Philip Markoff committed robbery and murder, that had nothing to do with his being a medical student," Welner said. "But it had everything to do with *him*. What aspect of him? There's nothing light that attaches itself to a predatory robbery and murder. What that darkness is in Philip Markoff is his secret."

31

Phil the Thrill

To understand just how driven the Craigslist Killer was during his seven-day frenzy, you need only examine the last time he struck—at the Holiday Inn Express in Warwick, Rhode Island. Dr. Casey Jordan, a criminologist and lawyer who speaks frequently at forensic psychology conferences around the country, explains why. "I don't believe he'd planned on killing [Julissa] at the Marriott," Dr. Jordan said. "But once it happened, he tried it again. He went out to rob again. That doesn't fit. Normally, after a murder, you'd see the guy go away and hide, lay low. Usually, the person is in a panic, but he wasn't. He went out and tried it again two days later. That indicates a rush or thrill beyond the rush or thrill he gets from sex."

Dr. Jordan believes the Craigslist Killer could not stop himself because he thirsted for greater and greater excitement. She calls him a "hedonistic killer" who also was interested in power and control. "The thrill is the primary thing," she said. "He evolved and blossomed. As one thrill fades, he needs something else to get that thrill. It needs to be something bigger and more violent. This guy's level of arrogance, the self-denial that he had to engage in to think he wasn't going to get caught, is baffling. The only way you'd be that careless is because the thrill is so great. It's as good as heroin."

And although the terms *sociopath* and *psychopath* often are thrown around casually, Jordan believes that this type of killer is not psychotic at all. "There is a character flaw here," she said. "A tremendous sense of self-entitlement, of privilege. It's a reflection of a new age in our culture, an unwarranted self-regard. These killers feel like everything should be handed to them. We especially see this in young white attractive men. He thinks, 'No one will ever believe it's me.' There's a level of false security that we've seen in the last five or ten years. A feeling that he's special."

And that brings us to Phil Markoff. Informed of the online profiles found on sexually explicit dating sites and his apparent interest in having sex with men as well as women, Dr. Jordan said it is possible that Markoff turned to armed robbery as yet another thrill. "After a while, gambling becomes boring, sex with men becomes boring. He needed something new. It's like an idea that doesn't have brakes on it," she said. "It is like a cancer."

The one surprise Jordan finds in Markoff's pathology is that he apparently was such a stupid criminal. "What's unusual about this guy is that most killers are smarter at the CSI issues," she said. "Usually, these people know about the cameras and know how to leave false clues. It's funny how the scummy guys know this, but this guy didn't. He left his fingerprints!"

Dr. Jordan said that the way Markoff allegedly behaved, "keeping the panties and the gun. That's part of the thrill. 'I have these things right here in my apartment.' The BTK Killer had souvenirs in a filing cabinet that was unlocked, that his wife could have opened at any time."

In fact, the BTK (which stood for bind, torture, kill) Killer from Wichita, Kansas, is in some ways a case reminiscent of Markoff's. BTK, aka Dennis Lynn Rader, was married to the same women for thirty-three years, raised a family, and was a leading member of a local Lutheran church. No one suspected his secret life as a serial rapist and killer until the day he was arrested for torturing and killing ten people. Part of the thrill for Rader was that he hid in plain sight, and once went so far as bringing a dead woman into his church after hours. He did it, he admitted, because of the thrill.

Says Jordan, "This guy [Markoff] was probably saying, 'I have everyone fooled. Look at how powerful I am. They would never dream of looking under my bed or in *Gray's Anatomy*.' There's a level of arrogance that trips up all the killers we catch. These guys really do think, 'No one would ever dream I'm capable of this.' And look at the statement by his fiancé. He knows this is what she thinks. She's a lamb to the slaughter. It emboldens him. If he can convince her . . . there is a level of self-brainwashing. 'If I can sleep in the same bed as my fiancée, who doesn't know, no one will know.' "

Police investigators cling to the idea that criminals are dumb, and Phil Markoff did not disappoint. He was book smart—brilliant, even—but he made a slew of mistakes that brought police literally to his front door.

And he was no smarter in Rhode Island than he was in Massachusetts. On May 4, 2009,

Attorney General Patrick Lynch and Warwick police chief Stephen McCartney announced they had issued an arrest warrant for Markoff—even though he was in the custody of the Boston Police—and were charging him with armed robbery and assault. Perhaps burned by the number of leaks to the press, the authorities chose not to detail their evidence. It hardly mattered, since newspapers had already reported that Markoff's fingerprint allegedly had been discovered in the stairwell of the Holiday Inn Express in Warwick, and that investigators allegedly could place him at the scene because of text messages. Both Amber, the exotic dancer, and her husband had been face-to-face with the killer, and if it was Markoff, they will be key eyewitnesses whenever this case makes it to trial. That could be a very long time, given that, first, Markoff will have to face charges in Massachusetts.

At the press conference to announce the arrest warrant, Lynch did not equivocate; he simply said that the person who attacked Amber and her husband at the Holiday Inn Express on April 16 "was Philip Markoff."

Buried deep in Lynch's remarks was a comment about the Internet and its ability to be used for good and evil. He repeated the usual warnings that "there are predators out there and we need to be aware," but then he said something that often is forgotten in the controversy over Craigslist and its apparent dangers. The Internet, Lynch said, "has blessed us all with a wonderful tool to exchange information."

In a story in which the web was made out to be the ultimate bogeyman, that simple statement was, at the very least, refreshing to hear said out loud.

32

The Grand Jury Returns

Except for his initial arraignment after he was arrested, Philip Markoff managed to stay out of public view. He ducked a second procedural hearing on May 21, and even two months after his arrest, no one had heard him speak a word. The case itself had fallen silent, but on Father's Day, June 21, that all changed. That Sunday afternoon, Jake Wark, the public information officer for Suffolk County district attorney Dan Conley, sent out an email with some breaking news—a grand jury had secretly indicted Markoff on first-degree murder, kidnapping, armed robbery, and other charges. His presence was required in court the following day to answer the indictment. Markoff could no longer avoid the spotlight.

The district attorney's office revealed new details of the attacks to the media, and they were even more damning than previous evidence. If true, the facts showed a troubling degree of premeditation, rather than the crimes of passion many had imagined. But as damning as the new details appeared, Markoff was still, in the eyes of the law, an innocent man.

The indictment alleged that in February 2009—two months before the Craigslist Killer began his crime spree—Markoff had purchased several disposable TracFone cell phones. The phones, which can be bought for as little as $9.99, do not require a service contract or any personal information before purchase, making them very difficult to trace. (The company slogan is "the cell phone that puts you in control.") The indictment alleged that Markoff used those phones to make contact with Trisha Leffler and Julissa Brisman. That would suggest not only foresight but also ingenious planning—if only Markoff had disposed of the phones! Incredibly, according to the indictment, he kept the phones after the crimes, and police allegedly found three of them in his Highpoint Circle apartment, including those used in the crimes. The receipts used to purchase the phones were also allegedly found in his apartment.

As had been revealed previously, police also allegedly found the murder weapon inside a hollowed-out copy of *Gray's Anatomy*, but for the first time it was revealed that the gun was a 9mm Springfield Armory XD-9 semiautomatic. Markoff allegedly bought it at the State Line Gun Shop in Mason, New Hampshire, with a driver's license that was not his. The license he used belongs to a New York State resident named Andrew Miller. Police interviewed Miller and

District Attorney Dan Conley later told reporters that investigators could not establish a connection between Markoff and Miller, nor do they know how Markoff obtained the license. The gun purchase was a sore point for Conley. He has often pointed out how easy it is to buy guns in neighboring New Hampshire, and this was a prime example, he said, because the name and photograph on the license Markoff allegedly used were not his, and reportedly Andrew Miller does not resemble Markoff. Allegedly, Markoff's fingerprints were found on the documents used to purchase the gun.

The indictment charged that Markoff hit Julissa twice in the head with the butt of that handgun after she resisted his attempts to rob her. "The blows to her head were so sharp and so violent that they fractured her skull," Conley said.

Criminalists found two bloodstains on the gun and a court ordered Markoff to supply a DNA sample.

There was more information revealed about

the panties allegedly found in Markoff's apartment. District Attorney Conley said four pairs of women's underpants were found rolled up in a pair of socks hidden in the box spring under Markoff's mattress. Two of the panties were identified by Trisha Leffler as hers, but Conley said police did not know the owner of the other two panties, except that investigators had established they did not belong to Markoff's fiancée, Megan McAllister.

The police also found a ball gag, similar to the type the Craigslist Killer used when he attempted to silence his Rhode Island victim. And they found several laptop computers inside Markoff's apartment, and said that, on one of them, they allegedly found "remnants" of the email communication between Markoff and Julissa.

On Monday, June 22, the case against Markoff shifted to Suffolk Superior Court and the seventh-floor courtroom of Magistrate Gary Wilson. Reporters and producers squeezed into the tiny courtroom. Each local television station had at least two on-air reporters in the room; it was standing room only. As usual in high-profile cases, only one television cameraperson and one still photographer were allowed to record the proceedings, but their video and photos were distributed, or "pooled," to the media. The Markoff family—Phil's father, mother, brother, and sister-in-law—sat huddled together in a back row near the window. The room was so crowded that reporters were forced to stand directly behind them, and could monitor virtually anything they said. Even whispers might be overheard, so the four of them said almost nothing for more than an hour as they sat waiting and watching. Markoff's mother rubbed her fingers together and stared at the door where her younger son would soon appear. Markoff's father tapped his umbrella nervously. Before the day was out, one particularly aggressive reporter stood over them and asked several times: "Do you believe your son is innocent?" They refused to take the bait, and said nothing. Another reporter looking on admired the family's courage in standing up for

Markoff in this sea of aggressive reporters, and said, "That's love."

The front row on the other side of the courtroom was roped off and empty. The hearing was set for 10:30 a.m., but at the appointed hour, nothing happened. Markoff was still absent from the courtroom even though his attorney John Salsberg and Assistant District Attorney Edmond Zabin were having a sidebar with Magistrate Wilson. Four court officers and a number of plainclothes police officers were in attendance. The courtroom had a small area partitioned off by a four-foot-high wall, where the defendants stand to hear the charges read against them. But Markoff was not there. Word circled through the media—the hearing would not start until Julissa's family arrived from New York. They were on their way.

And then, at about 10:50 a.m., Julissa's mother, Carmen, Julissa's younger sister, and a couple of other relatives walked in with a victim advocate who would translate the proceedings. The tape was removed from the front bench, and Julissa's family slid in. They were separated from the Markoff family by only a small aisle.

And then, at 11:01 a.m., Philip Markoff entered the courtroom. The assembled viewers fell silent—the sole sound was Markoff's leg irons dragging along the floor. Markoff took his place in the cordoned-off area reserved for defendants. It was only the second time he had appeared in public, and everyone was curious to note any change in his appearance. Markoff's blond hair was shorter, and he wore a white button-down shirt with blue stripes and tan pants. As it had been in his bail hearing, Philip's face was placid, though one reporter thought it looked as though he had aged ten years during his two months in custody. He never glanced toward his family or the rest of the audience. His eyes were locked on the magistrate and the court clerk, who would address him directly. Someone unfamiliar with the way the criminal justice system works might wonder why Markoff would plead anything but "guilty" in answering the charges, given all the alleged evidence against him. But very few defendants plead guilty at this early stage.

In a loud voice, the magistrate's clerk read the first-degree murder charge. He stood just a few feet away, and when he finished, he stared at Markoff and asked, "How do you plead to this indictment, sir?"

In a clear strong voice, Markoff answered: "Not guilty."

"Furthermore, sir, at this time, the grand jurors of Suffolk County return further six more indictments against you. Do you waive the formal reading of these charges, sir?"

"Yes."

"How do you plead to these six indictments, sir?"

"Not guilty."

Markoff was soon ushered out of the room, and the hearing ended. Conley, Salsberg, and others stood outside in the hallway, commenting on the proceedings. A lawyer representing Julissa's family read a brief statement expressing their sadness. And Phil Markoff's family was chased out of the courthouse and onto the street by reporters and camerapersons. The family never said a word. Behind the scenes, Philip Markoff sat in a holding cell before being taken back to the Nashua Street Jail, where he will be housed until his trial takes place, most likely in the summer of 2010. In a death penalty state, Markoff could plead guilty and forgo a trial in exchange for a life sentence, but that is not an option here. There is no death penalty in Massachusetts so there seems to be very little room for negotiation. Despite the mountain of apparent evidence, the case of the *Commonwealth of Massachusetts v. Philip Markoff* appears headed for trial. Having already lost everything, Markoff really has nothing left to lose. His freedom has been taken away, his medical schooling is in shambles, and his alleged dark side has been exposed.

Within hours of the hearing, it was revealed that Megan McAllister had testified before the grand jury in mid-June, reportedly to tell them she knew nothing of her former fiancé's alleged criminal activities. Her lawyer said she was in New Jersey from March 20 through April 18, and returned to the couple's Quincy apartment just as the police were putting it under surveillance. On that trip to Boston in mid-June, Megan made one more stop. She visited Markoff in jail and told him in no uncertain terms that she was no longer his fiancée and that she was moving on with her life.

The essential mystery that is Philip Markoff remains. If the evidence is correct, no one spotted his dual nature—on one hand an aspiring healer, on the other, a stone-cold killer. How can that be? DA Conley, a veteran of the criminal justice system, expressed no surprise. "The annals of criminal justice are filled with people who are able to compartmentalize their lives and fit in with society," he said matter-of-factly. "There are many instances like this—it happens."

Acknowledgments

First and foremost I would like to thank Daniel Sieberg, the CBS News science and technology correspondent who helped launch this book and who contributed to the sections on digital forensics and Craigslist.

Invaluable help in photo research and overall editorial content came from Sarah Prior, field producer for *48 Hours Mystery*, who contributed her reporting skills throughout the book.

As always, this book and the entire series of *48*

Hours Mystery books would not have been possible without the blessing of the program's executive producer, Susan Zirinsky, and CBS News senior vice president Linda Mason.

And thanks again to the guidance, goodwill, and understanding of the *48 Hours'* executive editor, Al Briganti, who ushers these books to publication.

Thank you to our legal counsel Nicholas Poser, who reads all the *48 Hours Mystery* books with a careful eye. And to Rita Dorgan for negotiating contracts.

And of course, thank you to the entire staff of *48 Hours Mystery*, who are talented, creative, and eager beyond belief, and who produced the program on the Craigslist Killer and every other program throughout the year. A special shout-out to Judy Tygard, Richard Barber, Cindy Cesare, Peter Henderson, Sarah Huisenga, Jud Johnston, Chris O'Connell, Peter Van Sant, and Michael Vele.

Paul would also like to thank his wife, Susan, and children, Alexandra and Peter.

Maria would like to thank her editors at the *Boston Globe,* particularly Jennifer Peter for always pushing her to pester her sources, a command that paid off in dividends, and Brian McGrory for his wise counsel. Maria would like to thank those people who talked to her for this story, but revealing their names would not really help them very much. Needless to say they know who they are and she is forever grateful for the trust and confidence they placed in her.

Finally, Maria thanks her fiancé, Michael, and her parents and her sister Victoria for their constant support.

Authors' Note

Some of the names in this book have been changed at the request of those involved. They are: Sarah, Julissa's former roommate; Monica, Julissa's close friend; Amber, the lap dancer attacked at the Holiday Inn in Rhode Island; Gary, the family friend of the McAllisters; Andrea, the young woman who attended school with Phil Markoff in Sherrill; Joseph, the classmate of Markoff's who explained how medical school operates; and Jill Stern, the witness who called hotel security after spotting Julissa Brisman lying in her hotel doorway.